ndy Gall

AGON
E MONEY NOW

tain in 1983 by
Limited
ndy Gall

Morgan, Stéphane
uig, to whom

y David Fuller
ower

039–2

haftesbury, Dorset
tain by
Chichester, Sussex
on Limited
omsbury Way
SG

Other books by Sa

GOLD SCOO
CHASING THE D
DON'T WORRY ABOUT T

First published in Great B
Sidgwick and Jackso
Copyright © 1983 S

Photographs taken by Charle
Thiollet and Jean-José
many thank

Illustration pages designed
Maps by John F

ISBN 0–283–99

Typeset by Tellgate Limited,
Printed in Great B
R. J. Acford, Industrial Estate
for Sidgwick and Jack
1 Tavistock Chambers, B
London WC1A

TO MASUD AND
HIS WONDERFULLY HEROIC
MUJAHIDEEN

Maps

Major Ethnic Groups of Afghanistan

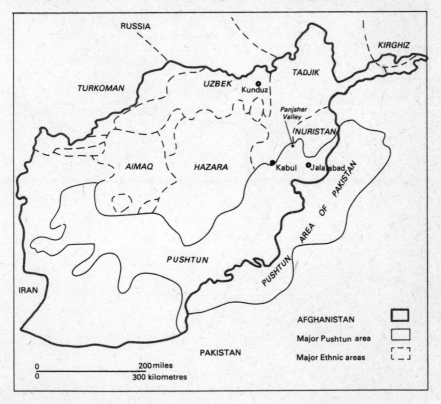

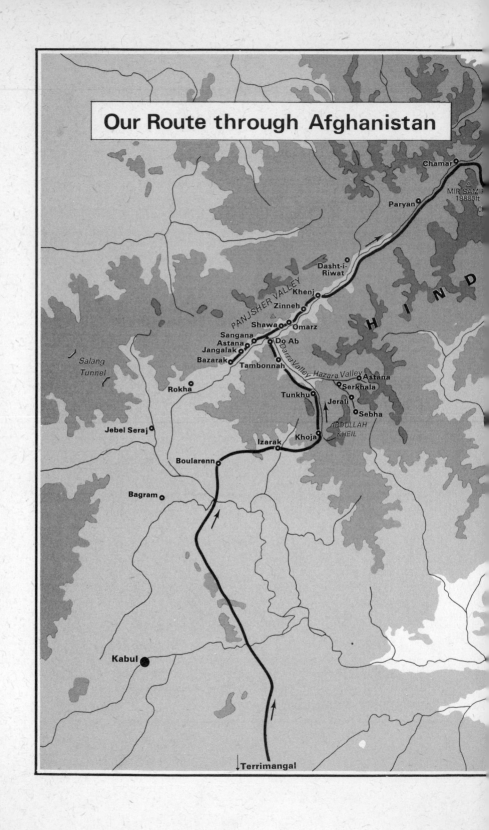

Our Route through Afghanistan

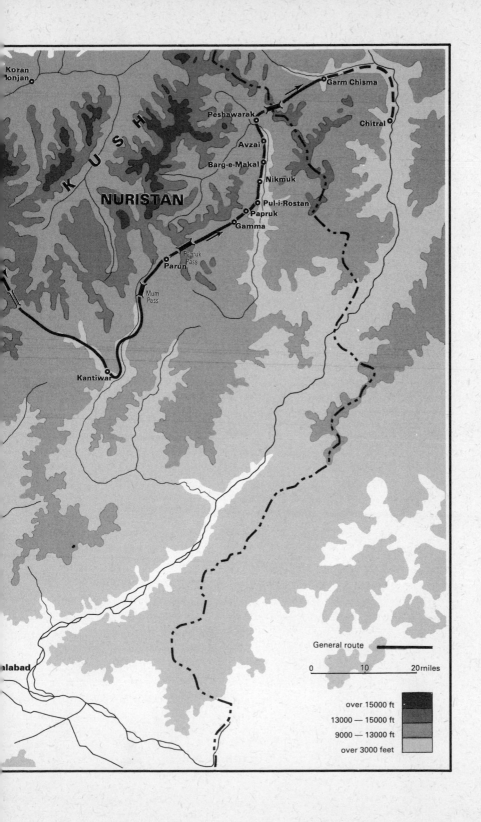

Koran
Monjan

K U S H

NURISTAN

Garm Chisma

Peshawarak

Chitral

Avzai

Barg-e-Makal

Nikmuk

Pul-i-Rostan

Papruk

Gamma

Papruk
Pass

Parun

Mum
Pass

Kantiwar

alabad

General route

0   10   20 miles

over 15000 ft

13000 — 15000 ft

9000 — 13000 ft

over 3000 feet

Behind Russian Lines

An Afghan Journal

1

'Where?' they said. 'Where did you say you were going? Afghanistan? You must be crazy.'

I said I probably was, but I was going anyway. Rather as for Richard Hannay in *The Thirty-Nine Steps*, life had lost its savour and I felt I needed excitement, a challenge. I had been flying a desk, as they used to say in the R.A.F., too long.

But Afghanistan was not just a personal adventure. The three-year-old war between the Russians and the Afghans was a very important issue that was being almost totally ignored, it seemed to me, by the Western media. The reasons were not hard to understand. It was a long way away, and therefore expensive to report both in time and money. Anyone who wanted to dig even a little below the surface would have to devote a minimum of two months to the project. True, scattered reports did emerge from time to time, but so far no one had tried to bring back anything like a comprehensive view of the war and of the Afghan Resistance. I felt it was high time someone tried to do it and who better qualified than myself? I had been a journalist for nearly thirty years, most of them as a foreign correspondent, and had covered more wars than I cared to remember. Not that I thought of myself primarily as a war correspondent: but every foreign correspondent finds himself reporting wars at some time or other and it is a necessary and useful training for any journalist who aspires to report one part of the world to another.

And then there was Afghanistan itself. Kipling called it 'that mysterious land beyond the Passes of the North', beyond the prize in the Great Game of espionage, played in the last century between Britain and Russia and described so brilliantly and romantically by Kipling in *Kim*: 'The Great Game,' he writes, 'that never ceases day and night, throughout India.'

This, then, would be a latter-day Great Game, played in the same part of the world; the North-West Frontier and, beyond it, the Hindu Kush, the ancient country through which Alexander the Great and Tamerlane had led their armies. The more I looked into it, the more convinced I became that this would be a great adventure, and maybe, the thought flashed through my mind, the last?

It was clear that we would have to go in the hard way, with the guerrillas, the mujahideen – the Resistance as they like to be called – running the gauntlet of a Russian army of occupation of 100,000 men, armed with helicopter gunships, jet aircraft and tanks.

Early on I consulted a friend, Charles Morgan, who had been a cameraman with ITN and now worked with an independent company. Charles is good-looking and dashing, as befits a young man whose father makes the Morgan sports car, and has something of the perpetual schoolboy about him. We had made a memorable trip together to Vietnam and Cambodia in 1980, and I wanted Charles to join me on the Afghanistan expedition. He agreed, and we flew to Paris several times to consult Jean-José Puig, a bearded and at first sight rather lugubrious French computer programmer, who knew a great deal about Afghanistan and the Resistance. He had spent most of the previous summer with the mujahideen in the Panjsher Valley, north-east of Kabul. He would prove invaluable for his local knowledge, so I was delighted he agreed to come.

Later I also enrolled Nigel Ryan, an old friend from Reuter days, who had been my editor at ITN and who had just left Thames Television. Nigel is one of the most attractive and intelligent men I know, as well as being very good company. We had been through a lot together, so our friendship was very strong. I knew his help would be tremendous, and he was instrumental in getting Charles Denton at Central Television to back us.

The final member of our group was Tom Murphy, a sound engineer and a colleague of Charles's. I knew very little about him except that he was twenty-two, London Irish, very good at his job, and had just been covering the war in Beirut for CBS. In fact, he returned just in time to buy his boots and the rest of his equipment for our journey.

So it was that on 1 August 1982, I found myself at London Airport with my four companions, clutching a ticket to Islamabad, the capital of Pakistan. Round our feet was piled a small mountain of luggage, about thirty pieces in all. Most of it was television equipment including a video camera, which Charles carried nonchalantly over his shoulder, and three video recorders, one of which Tom carried with equal insouciance. Both, I may say, were very heavy. We also had fifty tapes, which represented over sixteen hours of filming, and our own television monitor to view rushes on location.

Nigel arrived late with a duo of ladies, Annie Martin and Sabina, his faithful old Spanish retainer who calls him Don Santiago. Her fearful expression suggested that Nigel was about to canoe down the Amazon and end up in a headhunter's pot. The truth, although she could not know it, was to be almost as hair-raising.

Our plan was to walk in from the border between Pakistan and Afghanistan, which would take us, we estimated, a week or ten days. We would make contact with a guerrilla leader called Masud, who had been described to me as the Afghan equivalent of the young Tito, spend three to four weeks filming him and his fighters, and then walk back out. I estimated we should be back in London by the end of September.

One journalist, who had been in the Panjsher area earlier in the summer, had advised us to take some packets of soup, since the diet tended to be monotonous. So we had with us, among our array of equipment, a 'soup bag' containing fifty packets of Knorr soup, raisins, sweets and many bars of Kendal Mint Cake, so beloved of mountaineers and other travellers in remote parts of the world.

From the beginning I had tried to keep our trip as secret as possible, saying that I was going to take three months off to write a book. Now, with a huge pile of film equipment to explain away, we obviously had to change the cover story. We said we were going to make a travel film in Pakistan. As soon as we boarded the P.I.A. Jumbo, our inventiveness was put to the test, for, sitting on the opposite side of the aisle was an alert, friendly Pakistani who immediately recognized me.

'Ah, Mr Gall, where are you going this time? To another of your hot spots?'

I trotted out the line about a travel film, but Charles, sitting right in front of him, said, 'Oh, we might make a film in Swat.'

'Swat?' the man cried. 'Why, that's where I am from. If you come to Swat you must come and see me.'

One of the cabin stewards, overhearing the conversation, leaned over and whispered: 'That man is the Lord of Swat.'

Nigel immediately broke into verse: '"Who, where, why and what, is the Akond of Swat, Is he thin or is he fat, the Akond of Swat. . . ?" You know that, don't you? Edward Lear.'

I knew that the Swat Valley was supposed to be very beautiful, very high and with a rich culture of its own, but that was about all. A few minutes later, unable to contain his curiosity any longer, Nigel asked our travelling companion if he was the Akond of Swat. The man chuckled hugely.

'A-*hund* of Swat,' he repeated, correcting the pronunciation. 'No, no, the title no longer exists, but I am the great-grandson of the last Akond of Swat.'

Nigel found this intelligence fascinating and kept repeating 'Who, where, why and what. . .'. After that we settled down to our smuggled champagne – P.I.A. is officially dry – and pre-cooked dinner, flying direct from our one stop, Copenhagen, to Islamabad.

On a previous visit to Pakistan, I had been the personal guest of President Zia. This time I had deliberately not advertised our coming, but the discreet approach had its drawbacks. Instead of being met by a red carpet and an official car, we were left to flounder in a seething mass of disembarking passengers all trying to fight their way to the front of the immigration queue. The mêlée was made worse by the fact that, having reached the front and had our passports stamped, we had to turn round and struggle back the way we had come, breasting a tide of people all pushing and shoving.

As we regrouped near the baggage conveyor, the Akond of Swat's great-grandson reappeared and chatted for a few moments, while his baggage was briskly collected by his brother-in-law, the son of a former President of Pakistan, the late Field Marshal Ayub Khan. Our baggage took longer; the thirty pieces came trundling up the conveyor in ones and twos for the next twenty minutes.

When finally they had all arrived and been counted and recounted, the P.I.A. man who was meeting us led the way to Customs. This was the bit I was dreading. Pakistani Customs, like all Customs, can be extremely capricious and have the power to impose a huge bond, running into thousands of pounds, on camera equipment. Once before, I had fallen foul of an over-zealous customs

official – and that was when I was on my way to interview President
Zia. This time, if we got into trouble, there would be no powerful
friends to fall back on.

The P.I.A. man introduced us to an imposing gentleman in a
white uniform with navy blue epaulettes, the Customs Supervisor.
He listened to the story, then turned to me and demanded: 'Have you
got permission from Ministry of Information?'

'Permission? I did not know we had to have permission from the
Ministry of Information.'

'You must have letter,' he said testily. 'Without letter from
Ministry of Information, you cannot bring your equipment into
Pakistan.' His tone was that of a schoolmaster teaching a new boy
the twelve times table. For a moment our dialogue was interrupted
as other, more fortunate, travellers pushed their luggage towards the
exit.

At this point Charles Morgan came up and whispered in my ear,
'We've got three of the trolleys outside.' I was amazed. While we had
been going through the rigmarole of the letter from the Ministry,
Charles, Tom and Nigel had pushed three of the four heavily-laden
trolleys through the big doors at the end. In fact they had been waved
through by other customs officers anxious to clear the jam. The
Supervisor and the P.I.A. man, however, were quite oblivious to all
this. They had just agreed that the P.I.A. man would drive me to the
Ministry to obtain the necessary letter, and then bring me back for
the equipment. The Supervisor talked as if all this could be done in
the twinkling of an eye, but I knew very well it would take much
longer.

'As soon as you have letter, we release equipment.'

The Supervisor dismissed us with a lordly wave. But Charles was
at my elbow again. 'We now have the other trolley outside.'

Despite my excitement I kept my voice down. 'What, you mean all
the gear is now outside, all gone through?'

'Yes,' Charles grinned back happily. 'The whole bloody lot.' I
looked round carefully for the Supervisor. He was deeply embroiled
in some fresh problem. 'Let's go.'

We emerged into the blinding sunlight, pushing our way through
a throng of Pakistani taxi touts, trying to put as much distance as
possible between ourselves and the Supervisor. Unfortunately we
had taken so long that the minibus from Flashman's Hotel had
already departed, although the driver had promised to come back for

us. So we made our way to the far side of a pillar, piled our luggage on the ground, and prayed that the Supervisor would not suddenly reappear on his way to lunch. Our luck held. We never saw him again and when, forty minutes later, the Flashman's minibus drew up, we knew we were safely over the first hurdle.

The airport is half-way between Islamabad and Rawalpindi, an important garrison town in the days of the British Raj. Flashman's is a relic of those days: old-fashioned, unsmart, but clean and with a lot of character, even charm. After a hasty chicken sandwich and a cup of tea in the dining-room, we set off for Islamabad, fifteen miles away. Once clear of the chaotic traffic of Rawalpindi, we drove along a motorway planted with rows of pink and purple shrubs.

Islamabad consists mainly of ministries and embassies, a sort of garden city with acres of space between one building and the next. The effect is of a capital under construction, but the sense of space and greenness is attractive. The residential area is laid out in a grid system – the address of a friend was No. 4, 17th Street, in an area called F.62. The taxi driver never seemed to be able to find it. Beyond the city the hills begin, leading eventually to the higher and more formidable mountains of Afghanistan.

I had an appointment at the British Embassy, where an earnest, youngish man with spectacles was waiting for me. After some preliminary chat, he floored me by saying that both the northern and southern routes into Afghanistan were reported closed and we would therefore have to go in by the much higher and harder central route. He showed me on his map and my heart sank as his finger traversed a series of mountain ranges coloured palest brown and white. The white ones, I knew, were the highest.

I relayed the bad news to my companions waiting outside and, suitably depressed, we drove on in silence to our meeting with our mujahideen contact, Mohammad Es haq. He was staying at the villa of an Afghan doctor, set in a pleasant garden in a quiet back street. A good-looking man with a bushy beard, wearing a loose tunic and baggy trousers, Es haq came to greet us with a broad grin. He threw his arms round Jean-José and shook us warmly by the hand.

Was it true that the northern and southern routes were both blocked, we asked anxiously?

'No, no,' he replied, with what I was to discover was characteristic sang-froid. There had been problems but the southern route was now open and we would be going in that way in a few days' time.

Patience, he counselled, and all would be arranged to our satisfaction.

We left Jean-José to make the detailed arrangements and drove back to tea at Flashman's. Although I had met Es haq in Paris during the summer and brought him over to London specially to discuss our trip, I had never felt entirely at ease with him. He spoke excellent English and was the spokesman for the Panjsher Resistance, but I found him too glib and offhand. Secretly, I suppose, I resented the fact that he did not seem particularly impressed by my importance, appearing unable to differentiate between a responsible journalist like myself and some fly-by-night freelance who was interested in the Afghanistan war more as a personal adventure than as a serious piece of reportage.

In the evening Jean-José and Es haq set off to drive the hundred miles to Peshawar, once the old Afghan winter capital and later British headquarters for the North-West Frontier. All the Afghan Resistance groups have their offices in Peshawar and it was from there that we would eventually depart. But Es haq was anxious that we should not attract the attention of the Pakistani police, so he suggested that we should stay at Flashman's for a few more days. I thought, however, that we could keep the pressure on him better if we were in Peshawar, and therefore a couple of days later, we loaded all the luggage in a minibus and set off.

At first the road runs across a scrubby, deeply eroded plain, with a village or small town every few miles. Behind the screen of trees, we could see the whitewashed brick of the old British cantonments, now inhabited by the Pakistan Army. Lord Mountbatten, I was told, built a house here when he was Viceroy – no doubt to escape the heat of Delhi – but it cannot be seen from the road. At Attock the landscape changes dramatically. We climbed a small hill and suddenly the magnificent fort built in 1581, rose dark pink against the hot blue sky, its crenellated walls swooping down over a great outcrop of rock to the milky blue water of the Indus below. Attock marks the confluence of the Indus and the Kabul Rivers, and for a mile or so their streams, the Indus brown and the Kabul blue, run side by side before merging.

After Attock, the country becomes greener and more lush.Peshawar itself lies at the foot of the mountains in a humid depression and, when we arrived at lunchtime, it was blisteringly hot. It is a vibrant, untidy place with the excitement of the frontier about it. There are nostalgic relics of the Raj and in the great Bala Hisar Fort, which dominates the eye on arrival, glimpses of a past that goes back to Alexander the Great.

At the end of one dusty, tree-lined avenue, an oasis beckoned. This was Dean's Hotel, tin-roofed and single-storeyed, set in the middle of spongy green lawns. I had been there once before in December 1971, on my way to report the war between India and Pakistan. Then, to get to Rawalpindi, I had had to fly from London to Kabul, completing the rest of the journey by taxi over the Khyber Pass. I remembered the dining-room as lofty and gloomy but, although still gloomy with walls the colour of brown Windsor soup, a false ceiling had been added, which no doubt made the air-conditioning more effective, but gave the place a dismal, claustrophobic appearance.

Jean-José and a friend were finishing lunch. As we ate, Jean-José explained that a big arms' convoy would be leaving in the next few days and we would be going in with it. Es haq's organization, the Jamiat-i-Islami (the Society of Islam) would arrange for all our camera equipment to be taken across the border in advance and we would follow later. Charles did not like the idea of being separated from his camera, but Jean-José said the Afghans were adamant. They had their own methods of moving supplies across the border and we would have to trust them. No doubt our equipment would pass unnoticed among the guns and ammunition.

Es haq arrived that evening while we were having dinner. After a long conversation with Jean-José, he sat down at our table and launched into a long, fluent analysis of East-West affairs. He was highly critical of the devious games played by the French Trotskyists and Maoists, who, he said, twisted the facts of what was happening in Afghanistan and tried to mould the Afghan Resistance in their own leftist image. He was also extremely sceptical of the West's gullibility *vis-à-vis* the Soviets, advancing hard-line views that made Mrs Thatcher sound positively wet. But he did not strike me as a fanatic. Indeed, watching his handsome face with the dark, expressive eyes and Renaissance beard, and listening to his excellent English, I now felt that here was an eminently sane and sensible man: someone who knew what he was talking about.

Next morning Es haq returned as promised to inspect the camera equipment, accompanied by a black-browed, bristly-chinned bandit called Agha Gul, who looked positively evil until he smiled. He had been a policeman in Kabul until the invasion, when he returned to the Panjsher to join Masud. He was now Masud's chief of convoys, responsible for running guns and ammunition.

Agha Gul seemed unimpressed by the amount of equipment we had brought, which was a relief, and more interested in watching Charles demonstrate the incredible saddle he had had made in London. It purported to be a copy of an old Indian Army pack saddle, adapted to carry two of our three recorders, each of which weighed thirty pounds, and various other bits and pieces. Es haq held forth about the political situation in Kabul. The latest rumours suggested that Babrak Karmal, Moscow's puppet President, would soon be dropped by the Russians because of the failure of the summer offensive against the Panjsher. I asked Es haq who he thought would replace Karmal.

He answered contemptuously: 'Another slave.'

That afternoon, the Afghans returned to collect all the equipment, apart from our personal bags, loaded it up under the gaze of an inquisitive room-boy who was probably a police informer, and drove off with it. It was quite a wrench to see it go, soup bag and all.

There was quite a history to the soup bag. It was so heavy that when I picked it up at London Airport, both handles came off. It went missing on arrival at Islamabad and Nigel was obliged to make a special sortie on the morning we left for Peshawar to rescue it from the clutches of the Pakistani Customs. Then we were told by Es haq, via Jean-José, that there was no need to take any food with us, since the mujahideen would provide for our every want. Indeed, Jean-José said, it would be something of an insult to take our own food, implying that we did not trust our hosts. We debated the question long and seriously, finally arriving at the compromise that we *would* take the bag but offer its contents to the mujahideen *en route*. I watched the bag disappear into the back of the jeep with relative indifference: it was Nigel who was determined to bring it. Thank God he was, although even he could not have guessed then how heavily we would come to depend on the soups of Mr Knorr.

Things were clearly moving now, and Es haq departed saying it was time to fit ourselves out in the local costume. Accordingly, we told the hotel taxi driver, a breathy old boy with a slight shake, to drive us to the nearest bazaar where we each bought two pairs of long cotton shirts and baggy trousers. Mine were so wide round the waist that I could have got another person inside and still had room to spare. They were kept up by a cord, like pyjamas, and had no pockets. More seriously they had no fly buttons either, so to perform the simplest of bodily functions became quite an operation. The shirts also seemed to be designed for minimum usefulness, having only two breast pockets, too small to carry a wallet or passport. Still, as Nigel pointed out hopefully, they were cool and at least we looked a little less Western. We decided to put them on so that they would not look so new when we finally did set out, but when I clumped into the sepulchral dining-room in my enormous American Timberland boots, over-long shirt and clown's trousers, I felt and no doubt looked completely ridiculous. The remaining items were less ludicrous: a black and white chequered scarf like that worn by Mr Arafat of the P.L.O., which could be used as a handkerchief or towel, and a flat, woollen Chitrali cap.

Next day, 6 August, being Friday, the Moslem Sabbath, everything was supposed to be shut. But after breakfast we decided to walk the mile or so to the Peshawar Museum, which contains many fine statues of the Buddha, including one terrifyingly emaciated specimen known as the Fasting Buddha. There was also a small casket in which the Buddha's remains were supposedly preserved and which was found near Peshawar during the 1920s. Tom and Nigel took a taxi back to the hotel, but Charles and I decided to walk on over the railway bridge to the Khyber Bazaar, the city's main market. Ahead of us half a dozen horsemen were also crossing the bridge. From their turbans and long cloaks, they looked like Pathans, as fierce and proud as the horsemen of Genghis Khan.

The Khyber Bazaar was spectacularly busy. The main street teemed with horses, Vespa taxis, bicycles and pedestrians, overflowing into a warren of narrow lanes squeezed between stone and wooden houses, some of which were so close together you could step out of the upper windows into the room opposite. The drains were all open and the meat hung outside, but, despite the flies, the place seemed clean enough and prosperous.

There was order in the apparent confusion: each part of the bazaar was devoted to one activity. Thus there was a huge food section, subdivided into meat, spices, tea and so on; another for cloth, another for jewellery and another for tin trunks. Rows and rows of shops sold identical tin trunks of all shapes and sizes in what seemed to be a bad case of over-production. But this is the way of bazaars. Opposite the money-changers in the central square, a whole section was given over to leather ammunition belts and bandoliers:

hundreds of them hanging in thick rows, like *svelte* young snakes. Every now and again a group of Afghans would stroll up and demand to inspect a particular piece, perhaps a leather ammunition belt with a cross bandolier and shoulder straps costing 100 rupees (£5), rather cheaper than Holland & Holland. The war has created a boom for the Pakistani bazaar wallahs, although there has always been business here; the Pathans of the North-West Frontier have always enjoyed the right to carry arms. It is part of their birthright, rather as it is for the citizens of the United States.

We emerged from the bazaar behind the Bala Hisar Fort, its curious domes rising into the lapis sky like great brown nipples. It is built of brick, aged to the mellowness of old parchment, and its bulk broods benignly over the city, a reminder of past alarums and excursions. I could imagine British soldiers in their scarlet ceremonial tunics and topees, parading by the gate half-way up the hill, preparing for another foray against the border tribes. In those days we would have summoned a gharry to trot us back to Dean's. Now we squeezed into a three-wheeled Vespa. The two-mile journey cost us five rupees – twenty-five pence.

Next day we all repaired to the bazaar again to change money for the trip. Each money-changer had his own open cubicle, measuring four feet across by about six feet high, equipped with a wall safe. Nigel, as producer and thus in charge of finances, handed over a large wad of Pakistani rupees and was handed back an armful of Afghanis. The bazaar exchange rate was about a hundred Afghanis to the pound. I had calculated we would require about a thousand pounds for the six-week trip in Afghanistan, which meant we would need 100,000 Afghanis. But when I had done the sums the night before on the back of an envelope, I had miscalculated and Nigel found himself buying many more Afghanis than intended. It turned out to be a lucky mistake.

We were now as ready as we would ever be, kitted out with everything we could think of, including such miscellaneous items as flea powder, extra bootlaces and lavatory paper. Jean-José, looking thoroughly Afghan in his baggy trousers, with his bushy beard and dark Catalan looks, reported that we would probably be leaving on Monday the 9th, exactly a week after our arrival in Pakistan. That left one day free. So on Sunday morning, Nigel, Charles and I decided to play nine holes at the Peshawar Golf Club, which turned out to be very British and very empty. It was hot enough to induce a heart attack and after our exertions we collapsed on the clubhouse verandah where the steward brought us eleven glasses of fresh lime. Nigel and I drank four glasses each in rapid succession while Charles downed three. In the thirsty weeks ahead Nigel was to talk longingly about those fresh limes, as if they had been Château d'Yquem.

In the afternoon we took the hotel taxi to the Khyber Pass, driving past the mud-walled villages of the Tribal Area – a sort of no man's land in which the Pakistani Government, like the British before, has only nominal control. For example, if a man commits murder in the Tribal Area, he is safe from police action; only the tribal authority can bring him to justice. It was torridly hot, the sun beating back off the mountains, which are grey, shaly and extremely jagged. We stopped briefly at Landi Kotal, a wild-looking frontier town where a boy tried to sell me 'brown sugar' – half-refined heroin. This is one of the great entrepôts for heroin, which comes down from Afghanistan, is refined here and then shipped off to the West. In their attempts to curb the world sale of drugs, most of which end up in the United States, the American Government has tried to bring pressure to bear on President Zia to stop the traffic. But you only have to visit Landi Kotal and the frontier area to understand how difficult this is. The Pathans have always resented any interference in their lives, whether from Kabul or Islamabad. And, apart from their natural bolshyness, the money is irresistible.

Old Shakes, the driver, zigzagged us slowly up the mountain to the top of the Khyber Pass and we stood looking down on a patch of green five miles away. That was the border through which I had passed eleven years before but was now closed to us. The wind was cool as we shielded our eyes against the glare. It is a country made for bugles and the sniper, with crags everywhere. On every hilltop above the road the British had built a fort, although some of them looked more like tenements. The only really striking one, Shagai, a long, low brick pile, half fort, half prison, was built in 1927, the year of my birth. On the cliff face of the hairpins are displayed the insignia of the regiments that fought here among the rocks: Khyber Rifles, North-West Frontier Force, Royal Engineers and many others. On the hillside opposite Shagai, behind a couple of mud houses, we came across a forlorn little British cemetery, obviously long neglected, the graves unkempt. One or two of the flat burial stones were so badly eroded that we could not read the names, but the others all dated from 1919. Most of them had died of cholera.

That night after dinner, Nigel and I walked to the telex office to send our departure message to Charles Denton at Central Television. It said: 'Setting off tomorrow on time on budget.'

2

The jeep was supposed to come for us at 7.30 a.m. but, when we assembled in Jean-José's room, there was no sign of the mujahideen. Looking round, I suddenly realized that we had forgotten to buy our *pattus*, a light woollen blanket like a Scots plaid that also serves as a camouflage net against Soviet helicopters.

'Are they absolutely essential?' I asked Jean-José.

'*Ah oui, oui,*' he said. '*Absolument.* If you see a helicopter, you must lie down on the ground and pull the *pattu* over your head, like this.'

Charles and I took the hotel taxi to the Khyber Bazaar and in the space of five minutes had bought four handsome desert-brown *pattus* for £4 each.

We were back at the hotel shortly after eight and soon after that Agha Gul arrived in a small Nissan Land-Rover, painted as an ambulance. Our personal bags were stowed and we clambered in to what seemed a totally inadequate space. On one side sat Tony Davis, a young Australian journalist we had met for the first time that morning, Nigel, Jean-Philippe Tabard, a small French doctor with a big bushy beard, and Jean-José. On the other, Tom, myself, Charles and an Afghan. We had only gone a few hundred yards when I got acute cramp in my left leg, which was trapped awkwardly between Nigel and Jean-Philippe. With enormous effort, because of the weight of the Timberland boot, I managed to move it to between Nigel's legs. Then, too numerous and too large for this Oriental midget's torture chamber, we raced and bumped our way across the green countryside, hurtling through police checkpoints and villages at breakneck speed, scattering horsemen, pedestrians and chickens with fine abandon. Agha Gul, looking even more piratical than at our previous meeting, was squashed in the front beside another convoy leader, Gul Bas. The driver grinned hugely as he crashed into the potholes and Tom's head bounced painfully against the roof.

One very important person was missing – Es haq. At the last moment he had informed us, again via Jean-José, that the Jamiat – one of the half-dozen main resistance organizations – had received two visas for Saudi Arabia and he had been instructed to go there instead. I was annoyed and slightly apprehensive that we had lost our interpreter and escort, the one Afghan who knew who we were and what sort of film we wanted to make. None of our team had a single word of Persian, or Farsi as it is called in Afghanistan, and we had failed even to bring a dictionary with us. Luckily, however, Tony Davis had spent several months in Afghanistan the year before and had a working knowledge of the language.

After two or three hours of excruciating discomfort, we came to a small town called Parachinar, the Jamiat's forward base. The narrow main street was jammed with wild-looking Pathans all carrying rifles. We drew up at a big iron gate set in a high mud wall. Everyone was nervous and as soon as the gate opened we drove through quickly. Inside, there were about fifty young Afghans, each with a weapon, their backs leaning against the wall. They stared at us, but not in an unfriendly fashion, although we must have presented a strange sight. We were shown into the house at the end of the courtyard; they obviously did not like us standing about outside. There we were politely invited to sit down on one of the *charpoys* (beds) covered with rather dirty blankets and offered tea. These were the mujahideen we would be going with. Most of them were in their late teens or early twenties, and they all looked pretty tough.

An hour later we climbed back into the 'ambulance' with an extra passenger from the local Jamiat, who squeezed in beside Agha Gul. There was one more important checkpoint to clear and the escort instructed us to draw our P.L.O.-type scarves round our faces and pull our hats right down. But at the checkpoint the policeman did not bother to look inside the vehicle. Our escort got out and we drove off, arriving a few bumpy miles later at Terrimangal, a mud village perched on the edge of a ravine. Terrimangal is a very Kiplingesque caravanserai and is named after the two tribes who inhabit the area, the Terri and the Mangal. We drove through the village, bumping our way past what seemed to be the stables' area to the Jamiat's 'safe house'. Our temporary quarters were on the first floor, in a big room reached by an outside staircase, at the top of which were the alfresco kitchen and a rudimentary wash place.

Inside, hand-cut timbers supported the walls and roof and reminded me slightly of my own fifteenth-century cottage in Kent. From the little balcony we could look across the ravine to an encampment of nomads who make a living illegally hauling timber by camel, from just across the border into Pakistan. I wrote rather melodramatically in my diary that night: 'For the first time, I really feel at the beginning of the Great Adventure.'

We now became acquainted with a problem that would be part of our lives for the next two months. Our hosts did not use either inside or outside lavatories. They used nature. When I indicated that I wished to relieve myself, a young guerrilla beckoned me to follow him. We made our way between two houses, carefully avoiding the open drain, and walked across a flat piece of ground, past a large tethered camel, to the edge of the dried-up river bed. My guide pointed down the slope, indicating that I should clamber down until I found a suitable spot. He remained on guard above in case of trouble. I noted that for more serious operations I would have to cross the river bed to the cover of the bushes opposite.

On the way back, my young guide explained: 'Very bad men here. Everyone have gun. Very dangerous.'

That night, after a dinner of boiled rice and rather stringy, greasy goat, the first of many such delights, we lay down in our sleeping bags on the floor. It was uncompromisingly hard and I slept fitfully, vaguely conscious that I was being crawled over by a host of local residents. I woke feeling very stiff but unable to detect any bites. I also had a sore throat, and knew I was about to be ambushed by a bad cold. At six we breakfasted off tea and flat, round, unleavened bread, called *nan*. By 7.30 it was sunny and hot and I watched four young mujahideen, sitting cross-legged on the flat roof opposite, stripping, cleaning and reassembling what appeared to be brand-new Russian AK47 rifles, the weapon that helped the Vietcong to win the Vietnam War. They looked very expert.

We spent some of our time studying our surroundings with binoculars, but our hosts were nervous whenever we lingered on the balcony, pointing up the hill at the Pakistani police station about half a mile away. No foreigners are allowed in the frontier area without special permission, which is virtually impossible to get and, if we had been spotted, we would have been sent back to Peshawar. Naturally we all wanted to avoid that, so we complied reluctantly.

The day dragged until, in late afternoon, a lorry arrived with our equipment and the arms for the convoy. The shipment included a number of RPG7s, another well-tried Russian weapon which fires an anti-tank missile from the shoulder, and lots of cases of ammunition, including boosters for the RPGs and mortars. Now began an operation the unwieldiness of which made us marvel. Each piece of equipment was loaded on to a primitive scale and weighed against several stones which, they said, represented one Shir (7 kilos). There was no way of testing the accuracy of their Shir and no way of challenging their tally of our total weight, a horrendous 55 Shir (385 kilos). At 1,000 Afghanis (£10) a Shir, our bill to the Panjsher Valley 150 miles away was 55,000 Afghanis or £550. This was rather more than we had bargained for and we made them count it all again. But in the end, lacking any alternative method of weighing, we had to accept the Afghan figure. As soon as the pieces were weighed, they were carried off by one of the horse or donkey drivers and lashed on to a wicker panier as a load. As I gazed round at the motley collection of donkeys and horses, I wondered if they would ever manage to carry our heavy, fragile, and extremely expensive equipment across the mountains that lay in wait for us like so many bad dreams.

Before we went to bed, one of the local Jamiat worthies, a fine-looking big man with a thick beard, came to see us with Agha Gul.

'Do you need horses to ride?' he asked.

I looked round at my colleagues. 'No,' I said, 'I don't think so.' We had only budgeted for pack animals.

'We intend to walk in,' Nigel said very firmly, every inch the producer.

Agha Gul gave a leer which may have been his way of expressing polite interest but looked more like scepticism to me.

We got into our sleeping bags early because we were due to make a very early start. Indeed they woke us at one and I was up, dressed and outside by 1.30 a.m. The sky was dark, but the loading area between the houses was lit by oil lamps. The scene resembled a Rembrandt painting, a few pools of light surrounded by deep shadow, with faces and arms caught for a moment and frozen.

Agha Gul was perched on one of the flat roofs, keeping a cynical and watchful eye on the loading. Charles came up to me in some alarm.

'For God's sake, they're trying to load the camera on the smallest donkey in the place. It's absolutely ridiculous. We've got to stop them.'

I peered in the direction indicated. It was true. A very small donkey was being loaded not only with the precious camera, our one and only, but with other heavy pieces as well. I turned to speak to Agha Gul; thank God Tony was there to translate.

Agha Gul spoke sharply to the muleteers, but they ignored him, hauling away at the ropes on the little donkey. Charles was beside himself.

'You've got to stop them,' he cried. 'They're putting the most valuable piece of equipment on the smallest animal in the convoy. It's bloody crazy.'

I turned in desperation once more to Tony and Agha Gul. As I did so, the camera box and the rest of the load slipped right round under the donkey's body and fell on the ground. Even at two o'clock in the morning we had to laugh. The muleteer was incorrigible, trying to wrestle the load back again, but Agha Gul, urged on by me, set up a terrific barrage of imprecation from the flat roof. Finally, grudgingly, the donkey was led away and a horse brought. They were a terrible lot, I realized now, nearly all thin and dejected-looking, the victims of too much work and too little food. Poor brutes, they were the dregs of the Afghan horse world.

Charles was now busy wrestling with his special saddle, which was complicated to put on.

'This horse will never carry this load,' he finally declared. The two big recorders were slung on either side and other boxes were strapped on top and at the back. The horse they had chosen for this key load was scrawny and bad-tempered and, to show his displeasure, he lashed out with his hind legs. But it was only when he moved a few steps that we saw he would be lucky to get a hundred yards with that load. I went back to Agha Gul and remonstrated once more, waving my arms and shouting. After another noisy altercation, the scrawny beast was unloaded and, with a lot of dark looks and curses, another animal was found. It took us two hours to load. Finally at 3.30, with a half-moon coming up like a shy young girl, the order was given to move.

We started to walk uphill out of the village, the bells on the donkeys tinkling musically and the shouts of the drivers providing a sort of bass accompaniment. Dogs barked in the night and at one point a solitary cock crowed. The Pakistani police post glimmered ghostly white on the hill above us, but there were no lights and no signs of activity. I imagined that the Jamiat had done their bribing well. The half-moon gave us just enough light and at four we breasted the slope and saw on our left the ruins of the Afghan border post, long abandoned. We climbed steadily, overtaken by late-starting pack animals, and I began to feel the first weight of my small rucksack. The sky gradually lightened and, as we passed through a couple of border villages, the big mud houses, built like forts, were dark against the sky. Veiled women peered at us from doorways and old men shouted directions. Some of these border villages are not very friendly to the Jamiat and our mujahideen did not delay, pushing on steadily upwards, until the villages were left behind.

By nine the sun was surprisingly hot as we plodded on past one or two wrecked Russian personnel carriers, old burnt-out wrecks from the early days of the war. The hillsides were ravaged and bare, all the timber cut and dragged away. The convoy was now strung out over at least a mile and we settled down to a fairly steady rhythm. But the valley was growing narrower and ahead we could see the path climbing up a steep hillside. At the top, a long way ahead, lay the first pass.

As I trudged up the first steep part, my heart began to hammer and my lungs to labour. Two young mujahideen in black leather jackets, one of them carrying an RPG, encouraged me with smiles. They talked to one another all the way up the accursed slope, as if they were out for a Sunday afternoon stroll. But I found it increasingly difficult to resist the temptation to stop. At one point a black redstart, an incredibly handsome bird about the size of a sparrow, perched on one of the juniper bushes beside the trail. Despite my exertions I was filled with momentary pleasure, but had no spare breath to announce my discovery.

At the top of the hill we came on our first *chai khana* (tea-house), a scruffy-looking mud hut. Inside, it was dark and smoky and filled with villainous-looking ruffians. Despite this we sat down with an enormous feeling of satisfaction. Charles and I were offered tea by a mujahidin in a leopard-spotted combat uniform, who had recently returned from six months' training in Iran. Like nearly all Afghans, he had perfect manners. He served us first, offered us some of their hard biscuits and kept filling our cups as soon as they were empty. We were both so thirsty that we must have drunk five or six small cups of sweet green tea in rapid succession. I found it an effort to get to my feet and hoist my rucksack onto my back again.

From here the climb was easier and then came a long-striding swing down. I was sneezing about every ten minutes and my handkerchief was soaking wet. I felt both sorry for myself and intensely irritated that I should have caught a heavy cold at this of all times. I tried to be philosophical, without much success. In mid-afternoon, with the temperature in the nineties, we came to a small group of houses and stopped for a rest. There was a young man with us, an officer I guessed, who said he had been studying engineering at Kabul University when the Russians invaded and the war had started. Being educated, he could speak Pashtu (the Panjsheris are Persian speakers) and was able to order tea from a small boy. The samovar was lit and we lay there in delicious anticipation. The boy's sister, a pretty girl of about ten, peered at us from the field above, flirting with Nigel. In a year or two she would be behind the veil for good. But where was Tom?

'He was having trouble with his legs,' Charles said. 'But the muj were with him.'

Tom arrived about an hour later, hobbling and obviously in pain. Luckily Jean-Philippe was on hand.

'He has cramp,' he announced after one glance. 'He must have salt and he must bathe his legs in the river.'

As nearly always in Afghanistan, we were within a few yards of a river. Jean-Philippe helped Tom take down his baggy trousers and massaged his thighs, splashing cold water on them to ease the cramp. But it was clear that Tom would be unable to walk much further.

'He must have a horse,' Jean-Philippe declared. We still had some way to go to the place where we were due to spend the night and it must have been agony for Tom.

When we finally reached the village, we found Gul Bas, the second-in-command, and his men ensconced in the local 'hoteli', which, needless to say, bears no relation to what Westerners understand by that name. In the yard in front of the mud house, thirty or forty men were waiting for their first meal of the day. Bread was being baked in a big earthenware oven sunk in the ground, the bottom full of a glowing red wood fire. The baker squatted on his heels, reaching down to smack the thin, flat, oval-shaped *nan* against the side of the oven, where it stuck and cooked. His right arm was protected by a thick strip of cloth wound round the forearm, but it looked a hazardous operation. His assistant, hovering on the other side of the furnace, extracted the bread when it was cooked, peeling it off the wall with a wooden fork and hoisting it dexterously through the narrow mouth of the oven.

We were to sleep in the big communal room already occupied by about a dozen other men. It looked a good ambush position for the local army of fleas and bed bugs. But I was troubled by a more serious matter. The horses and all our equipment were elsewhere and, if we were to get a horse for Tom, who was by now hardly able to walk, something would have to be done tonight. Reluctantly I decided I would have to walk on to where the horses were camped. Nigel said he would come with me. I imagined that Gul Bas would send an escort with us, but he decided to take us himself, and after a vile supper of tough goat and rice, we set off in the gathering dusk. It was a long hike through a series of villages. Unseen but viciously snarling dogs menaced us from the tops of walls. Gul Bas would pick up a stone and once, when the dog sounded particularly aggressive, he cocked his AK47. But apart from Tom, I was worried about our camera equipment. We had been warned that we would probably get separated from the horses and here we were, on the very first day, miles away from our baggage, with the added complication that the man looking after the camera horse did not know how to load Charles's Indian Army saddle.

We walked for one hour, then another, following the dim shape of Gul Bas and the two leather-jacketed muj, who seemed to feel no fatigue and could apparently see in the dark. The last stretch was steep and Nigel and I slipped and stumbled blindly and painfully down the rocky slope, cursing with irritation and exhaustion. We reached the encampment at around ten, the drivers' lamps making pinpricks of light in the darkness. Gul Bas found Jamil, an irascible black-eyed brigand with no thumbs, only fingers, who was in charge of the horses. It was impossible to make him understand that we needed a horse for Tom, but at least we were able to make sure that our equipment was all there. We must have been a bloody nuisance stumbling around in the dark, tripping over sleeping drivers and insisting on opening various bags, but the Afghans were remarkably patient.

Eventually we were told we could sleep on the roof, and were helped to clamber up in the dark. Tea was handed up and Nigel and I chose our sleeping positions. There was not much room – it was a pretty full roof, with Jamil ensconced at one end. I found a space for myself right on the edge, fifteen feet above the ground. I unrolled my sleeping bag, climbed in cautiously and stretched out with a feeling of utter relief. For a moment I lay on my back gazing up at a skyful of stars. They seemed close and very bright. Then I turned on my side. Not even the hardness of the roof against my hip could hold up sleep now.

Next morning we had just had our tea and *nan* when the others arrived, Tom on the top of a horse, looking much happier. Somehow, this had been arranged overnight so last night's trek had been largely unnecessary. But there was a new problem. Charles's legs were giving out too and he said he did not think he could walk much further. Urgent discussions followed, but it was difficult to get any sense out of Jamil who was beside himself, rushing about to see that the drivers loaded properly and got off on time. We finally extorted a promise of a horse for Charles 'on the far side' of the river we now had to cross. It was about fifty yards wide and fast-running but only knee-deep. I kept my boots on and squelched my way up the slope.

It was a beautiful morning, the sky a cool, pale blue and the mountains russet-coloured, almost completely bare and very stark; but the most striking thing of all was the light, so pure and shining as to be crystalline. It enhanced everything, every bush, every stone, every flower. I decided to walk with Charles who was hobbling, but quite gamely and at a steady pace. We climbed for an hour or two and then made a long descent down a very eroded hillside, the water-courses twisting like snakes far below us. Eventually, our throats parched, we saw what we thought was a tea-house in the distance at the foot of the long slope, by the side of the river. We could see horses, and men sitting on the grass in the sunshine outside the hut, and the thought of hot, sweet tea beckoned us powerfully. Nigel was waiting at the bottom. He had rushed on ahead to catch up Jamil and get the horse promised to Charles. When he finally did catch him, Jamil had been extremely rude.

'He just shouted at me, and rode off, on Charles's horse. What a bloody rude man he is.'

Once again I bitterly regretted the absence of Es Haq, but with Jamil's disappearance, there was nothing for it but to watch Charles struggle on, getting steadily lamer. After a mercifully flat stretch we arrived in a village in early afternoon to find most of the muj and the horses resting by the river. Jamil was running about looking extremely important. We approached him tactfully through Tony, but he seemed to have forgotten his tantrum with Nigel. A bargain was struck with a local man to hire his horse for the remainder of the journey for 6,000 Afghanis (£60). Jamil negotiated the deal, so we had doubts about its straightness, but I was hugely relieved to have solved the problem of Charles's transportation.

I wrote in my diary that night:

The march begins to become one long blur of acute hardship going uphill (although I think even after two days I'm getting fitter, despite my cold), bliss at reaching the top of the pass, a moment of delight taking in the fantastic mountainscape, then the plunge downhill, almost as hard as the uphill. The best moments come when the path smooths out and you walk along the irrigation channels, the water bubbling deliciously in the heat, the maize tall and green, the walnut trees and mulberries casting deep pools of shade in an otherwise bare landscape. Parts remind me of Greece, but there are no olives here. The small pleasures – pink mulberries, apples, small apricots, a cup of sweet green tea – are hugely satisfying. . . . The evening light now is serenely beautiful, the wind bending the willows, the country apparently at peace.

3

We started at six the next morning. It's extraordinary how quickly old habits die and new ones are forged. As someone who usually goes to bed rather late, I was really enjoying going to bed early and getting up early.

We climbed straight up a steep, red hillside. The mountains were rust and green – perhaps there is a lot of iron in the rocks. A thin line of mujahideen marched, ant-like, up the mountain ahead of us. To my surprise, Jean-José turned out to be the worst walker: perhaps because he is a heavy smoker. He cut an eccentric figure, clutching his *canne à peche* (fishing rod) in its canvas cover like some magic wand.

The muj are exceedingly tiresome in the way they shout '*Arakat*' (move on) and '*Bala*' (up) at you whenever you show signs of falling by the wayside. Jean-José climbed the first steep stretch very, very slowly with a young guerrilla walking right behind him, urging him on. Every time Jean-José stopped, the young man would shout '*Arakat*'. Suddenly Jean-José, usually the most controlled of men, lost his temper.

'*Non, Non,*' he shouted with stentorian emphasis, drawing himself up at the side of the path. Then, bellowing like an angry bull, '*Passe! Passe!*' The muj finally took the hint and went on, leaving Jean-José to make his painful progress up the path alone.

After an hour or so we emerged into a huge rocky bowl to find ourselves walking through drifts of wild lavender, the pale purple flowers covering the dun hillsides in great profusion. I crushed some between my fingers; it was deliciously fragrant, although less strong

than English lavender. As we walked across the bottom of the bowl
we heard our first Russian jet, but so high as to be invisible. A little
later we heard the different beat of a helicopter or possibly a slow
fixed-wing aircraft, but again it was so high as to be out of sight.

At the far side of the bowl, the path climbed steeply up to the
saddle, partly hidden in mist. Half-way up we padded through
another field of wild lavender, disturbing a small flock of finches or
pipits, and what looked like a redstart. It was a long climb, although
not quite as exhausting as I thought it would be. When we reached
the top, we could see range on range of brown mountains, stretching
far ahead of us, like waves on the sea. Apart from Gul Bas, the rather
lackadaisical second-in-command of the convoy, the party included
two young brothers, one rather pock-marked, whom I rated as
second lieutenants and twenty or thirty 'other ranks' including the
two lads in leather jackets with Kung Fu written on the back and
short haircuts, a sure sign that they had recently deserted from the
Army. They were all equipped with new AK47s and RPGs.

By nine we had cleared the pass and were at the head of a fertile
valley which we descended at speed and in eager anticipation of tea
and food. The path now followed an irrigation channel, about two
yards wide and a foot deep, carrying a fast-running stream of
beautifully clear water. Every ten or twenty yards, leading off the
main channel, a crystal jet of water would splash down into the fields
of ripening maize and wheat. The constant sound of running water
became a delightful but tantalizing accompaniment to our march:
however clean they might look, to drink from the irrigation channels
was a sure way of catching a dose of diarrhoea or worse.

After an hour or two we reached a small village of mud houses, the
high walls looking shuttered and defensive. We stopped to rest under
a mulberry tree, its matt green foliage casting a big patch of shade. I
sat with my back to the trunk and looked up. The branches were
covered with pinkish white berries about the size of a raspberry and
very sweet. A mujahid climbed the tree and shook the boughs until
the mulberries fell all around us like manna: I gorged myself until I
felt slightly sick. I remembered from school that in China silk worms
are fed on mulberry leaves, but we never saw a single silk worm in
Afghanistan. Just before we set off again, we heard the sound of
another jet and, although it was a long way away, I felt a small
twinge of fear.

We marched on, reaching the large well-built village of Tizeen at about eleven. There was a spring in the middle of the village, with a jet of clear, cold water which we drank greedily. Tizeen boasted three shops, although it was hard to recognize them as such, since they had neither signs nor anything in the windows. Two were closed but inside the third a young boy was weighing out sweet biscuits for the mujahideen. We bought some too, and raisins, which in Farsi go by the delightful name of *kish-mish*. As we sat eating our biscuits, a villager strolled past us munching apricots and immediately offered us some – a typically Afghan gesture of hospitality. They were sweet and juicy and we devoured them hungrily.

Beyond the spring, a doorway led into the courtyard of the mosque, shaded by two magnificent plane trees. The mosque itself, a modest whitewashed mud and timber structure, stood on one side of the courtyard; the stream, where the faithful washed before prayers, ran down the middle and on the other side, partly shaded by the plane trees, was a gravelled courtyard. Having taken off our boots, since this was considered holy ground, Nigel and I spread our *pattus* in the shade at one edge and lay down to rest. Tony Davis was busy writing up his notes and poor Jean-José was, as usual, miles behind. Charles and Tom had taken a different route with the horses and we would not see them until the next stop.

We were roused to wash and have lunch, *nan* shredded into small pieces and dunked in a mixture of oil and yoghurt. It was extremely welcome, although messy to eat with the fingers.

Tizeen is surrounded by a series of hamlets that spill down the hillside like those fortress-cities in medieval Italian paintings. The mountains are magnificent, range on range of them, brown, purple, rust, ochre, stretching into the far distance. Half-way down the valley we were halted by vague rumours of fighting ahead. Certainly, we could hear the drone of what I took to be a spotter plane. A bee-eater or shrike, the butcher bird which impales its victims on thorns, with strong bill and vivid grey and black markings, perched for a moment or two beside us as we waited in the shade.

After twenty minutes, the order to move was given – '*Arakat*' – and we struggled to our feet and marched on, fortunately downhill. Despite all my walking and jogging before departure, my feet were getting the apparently inevitable blisters. The path followed the irrigation channels, lined with tall blue daisies, like cornflowers: the blue flower of the Afghan Resistance Movement, as opposed to *die blaue Blume*, the blue flower of the German Romantic Movement, of

Clemens Brentano and Heinrich Heine. The mind spins on endlessly, like a perpetual-motion top, as one walks, maintaining a sort of internal monologue. I was beginning to know the pattern of my thoughts as they reflected the conditions of the march; toiling uphill I thought constantly of sex and cool drinks, especially Buck's Fizzes and Bellinis. On the gentler stretches, I would occasionally think nobler thoughts and have enough detachment to admire the spectacular scenery and the bird life.

Late in the afternoon, the valley broadening now to a wide, dried-up river bed, with the stream a mere slender rush of water in the middle of the stony expanse, we came to a small oasis, a patch of mulberry trees where the horses had stopped. Charles and Tom had unsaddled and were reclining on what looked like a heap of horse dung. As we subsided among the dung and stones, we immediately asked for tea.

'No tea,' said Tom. 'There's no water.' Nigel and I groaned with irritation and exhaustion and would, no doubt, have spent the next half hour discussing how to organize a cup of tea, if a sudden altercation had not erupted unexpectedly fifteen yards away. The irascible thumbless Jamil, the horse-coper, was involved in a furious argument with a young mujahid. Apparently Jamil had ordered some of the mujahideen, including this young man, to carry on down the valley and they had refused. In the argument that followed Jamil had grabbed an AK47 as if he were going to shoot the young mujahid. The latter, insultingly cool, also seized the weapon and wrestled with Jamil. As they lurched backwards and forwards, the mujahid easily holding his own and Jamil's dark gypsy face becoming more and more contorted with rage, Gul Bas and the others tried to intervene. But Jamil was uncontrollable, screaming threats, his black eyes flashing with rage. The muj were clearly embarrassed by our presence and sheepishly asked us to move on. We left them, still at one another's throats, and set off down the valley.

We walked for an hour across the stones of the dried-up river bed, eventually stopping by a small wood. We pitched camp in a meadow, shaded by a line of fluttering silver willows. After some time a man arrived from the nearby cluster of houses with a samovar and proceeded to boil water and make tea. We all had a raging thirst and gulped down cup after cup of sweet green tea, called *sabs*. Next the man brought apples and we bought several kilos. They were delicious; extremely juicy and, apart from the apricots and mulberries, the first fruit we had had since we left Pakistan. In Britain, no doubt, they would have tasted quite ordinary. But here, by the side of the river, after a long hot day's march, our senses sharpened by exertion and fatigue, they were, I thought, the best apples I had ever eaten. I must have consumed a dozen, one after the other, at great speed.

Just before sunset, when the light was wonderfully pure and gentle, and the whole landscape hushed, we heard the rumble of a petrol engine. To our surprise a captured Russian jeep came bumping towards us with two grinning mujahideen inside. They drove up the river bed and back, like boys with a new bicycle, and then disappeared. After supper we wrapped ourselves in our *pattus* and tried to sleep on the hard ground. Because of the Jamil tantrum we had become separated from all our baggage and so had no sleeping bags or toilet things. It was a miserable, cold night.

Next morning Nigel and I insisted on going back to the horses to look for our personal things. Gul Bas came with us, a man of few words even in his own language. While Nigel and I tried to collect everyone's belongings together, Gul Bas went through the arms inventory, ticking off the numbers of rockets (rak-et), RPGs and Dashakas (Russian-made DSK heavy machine guns) while the horses and donkeys chewed placidly under the mulberries.

As we unpacked our medical supplies, a boy with a big cut on his knee which had almost healed begged for treatment. I gave him some ointment, then everyone else crowded round wanting attention. The mujahideen had to shoo them away, while we kept repeating, as emphatically as possible: 'Doctor ne, doctor ne. . .'. Jean-Philippe, the French doctor with us, said that the villagers had not seen a doctor since the war started. According to him there were only about thirty doctors in the whole of the liberated areas, that is to say the areas under the control of the Resistance (ninety per cent of the country), all of them foreign and most of them French. There were usually two or three French doctors in the Panjsher Valley, although at the moment there was none. There had been two French women doctors until recently, but when the Russians launched their big offensive against the Panjsher in the summer, they had kept asking in every village they took where the French doctors were. Masud became convinced they were trying to capture them for propaganda purposes (as happened to Dr Philippe Augoyard in January 1983) and gave orders for them to be moved to safety outside the main valley. A rival guerrilla leader, Gulbuddin, was also deliberately stirring up trouble by accusing Masud of sleeping with Western 'whores' so, reluctantly, he decided to send the women doctors back to France and stick to men for the time being.

We had only just walked back to the wood at 1.30, when we heard the sound of helicopters, not far away. The muj became very jumpy, shouting at us to take cover in the wood. We could hear jets as well. Then the helicopters started bombing. Although it was two miles away, the sound was very loud and frightening. There were three or four big explosions, the crack of rocket fire and the curious, almost obscene noise of the MI-24's machine guns which fire a thousand rounds a minute. It is a deep, almost animal, sound, like the growl of a prehistoric monster. Every time I tried to move to see what was going on, the muj shouted at me to take cover, although the helicopters were so far away they could not possibly have seen us. I could only conclude that these muj had little or no battle experience and that surprised me. Leopard Spots, the muj who was just back from training in Iran, was the jumpiest, and the coolest a sixteen-year-old boy with his own brand-new Chinese-made AK47. After ten minutes, an MI-24 flew directly over us on its way home and we emerged to see smoke and dust still hanging in the air further up the valley. I was extremely worried that they had been bombing the other camp, where the horses were, and I had a sudden terrifying vision of the camera gear being blown to smithereens. But it turned out that they had blown the village where we had had lunch the day before, killing six people.

We had often wondered why the Russians had not attacked our convoy, which always seemed so vulnerable as it straggled over the bare hills. They must have known about it, one imagined, both from their spies in Peshawar and along the way. There was no doubt that some of the Pathan villages in the border area were either hostile to the Resistance for tribal reasons, or else were being bribed to supply information by the Russians, working through the Karmal regime in Kabul. There was even the occasional battle. This sort of feuding, reminiscent of the Campbell-MacDonald hatred that led to the Massacre of Glencoe, is perhaps the most unattractive feature of the Afghan character. Why do highland people seem more prone to this sort of treacherous bloodletting? Is it to do with their claustrophobic, valley-bound world? One wonders if in some curious way it is the reverse, an aberration of the cult of hospitality, by which all Afghans live, just as the Highlanders did in the Scottish glens.

In the days of the Raj, the British had always intensely admired the Pathans of the North-West Frontier. They were great fighters and great gentlemen, even if they were the enemy. We had taken Kipling with us and I re-read *The Ballad of East and West*:

> *Oh, East is East, and West is West, and never the twain shall meet,*
> *Till Earth and Sky stand presently at God's great Judgement Seat;*
> *But there is neither East nor West, Border, nor Breed, nor Birth,*
> *When two strong men stand face to face, though they come*
> *from the ends of the earth!*

The two strong men, of course, are a British colonel's son and Kamal, a Pathan chief, who steals the colonel's mare. The son sets off in pursuit across the desolate hill country: 'There is rock to the left, rock to the right, and low lean thorn between. . .'. Eventually, the son's horse falls, but Kamal, who could have killed him, spares his life and they end up, improbably perhaps, pledging undying friendship across the cultural divide – more than friendship, blood brotherhood:

> *They have looked each other between the eyes, and there they found no fault.*
> *They have taken the oath of the Brother-in-Blood on leavened bread and salt;*
> *They have taken the oath of the Brother-in-Blood on fire and fresh-cut sod,*
> *On the hilt and haft of the Khyber knife, and the wondrous names of God.*

Finally Kamal sends his son back to serve in the Guides, one of the crack cavalry regiments of the British Army in India.

> *With that he whistled his only son, that dropped from the mountain-crest.*
> *He trod the ling like a buck in spring,*
> *And he looked like a lance in rest.*
> *'Now here is thy master,' Kamal said,*
> *'Who leads a troop of the Guides,*
> *And thou must ride at his left side*
> *As shield on shoulder rides.*
> *Till death or I cut loose the tie,*
> *At camp and board and bed,*
> *Thy life is his – thy fate it is*
> *To guard him with thy head.*

So, thou must eat the White Queen's meat,
And all her foes are thine,
And thou must harry thy father's hold
For the peace of the Border-line.
And thou must make a trooper tough
And hack thy way to power –
Belike they will raise thee to Ressaldar
When I am hanged in Peshawar!'

A nice dig, that last line, at the perfidious British.

In his classic work on the Pathans, Sir Olaf Caroe describes the Pathans' elaborate tribal code of honour, which the British found so close to their own public-school way of thinking. But we were approaching the subject from an entirely different point of view. According to Jean-José, the Pathans had given the Afghan Resistance a bad name, letting their own petty squabbles get in the way of the more important work of fighting the Russians and giving foreigners the impression that no Afghan could be trusted to do anything except follow his own personal advantage. Again, the sort of criticism that used to be levelled at the old Scottish clans.

Because the Pathans occupied the southern half of Afghanistan and since most Western journalists made only short trips across the border in the south, Jean-José argued, they inevitably drew false conclusions about the Resistance. It was essential to go further afield, to the east and north, where we were going, to Tadjik country, in order to understand that the Resistance could be very different and that all Afghans were not like the Pathans. The biggest single difference in their character, Jean-José claimed, was that whereas the Pathans loathed discipline of any kind, the Tadjiks took more kindly to it, especially if it came from a man they recognized as their leader. And that, we were told, was what Masud had achieved.

After the helicopters had passed and the horses had caught us up, we set off at a rapid pace down the valley, passing a group of nomads with their camels and dogs. They had pitched camp beside the river and we saw their women, darkly beautiful, moving between the tents, apparently less given to the veil than the Pathans. One man, with a fierce-looking moustache, came to stare at the file of guerrilla fighters and no doubt at us, the infidel foreigners.

After a long hike down the valley we branched off and started to climb between arid hills, Gul Bas keeping up a stiff pace. He explained through Tony that there were two forts ahead, occupied by enemy soldiers, and we would be in their field of fire. So we would have to keep together and walk fast. As an added incentive, Jean-José pointed out that we were near Gandamack, where in the first Anglo-Afghan War in 1842 the remnants of the British column retreating from Kabul made their last stand and were cut down pitilessly. One officer, Captain Souter of the 44th, who saved the regimental colours by tying them round his waist, and a few privates were taken prisoner. Of the five-thousand-man army which left Kabul on 6 January 1842, only one man, Surgeon Brydon, was to get through to the garrison at Jalalabad. Even now, in high summer, it was a desolate, forbidding place, but in winter, in deep snow and with the wind howling off the hills, it must have been a dreadful place to die. We toiled up a steep bare hillside, conscious that we would be very conspicuous to any observer and half expecting to hear the crack of a rifle or the thud of a mortar.

About dusk, at the start of the downslope which led eventually to the Kabul River, we came on the two forts, mysterious in the half light, their mud walls as bleached as the sand and rock around them. We marched past in silence, keeping a nervous eye open for any activity, but the buildings must have been empty – or the soldiers asleep. One fort, right beside the path, was badly damaged, suggesting that it had been attacked in the past by the mujahideen. Certainly a handful of soldiers sitting up there on the top of the mountain would have been a tempting target, as vulnerable as we were now.

As darkness fell we began the long trek towards the river. At first the going was easy, a white sandy path that wound in and out of the small prickly bushes of camel thorn, but as we went lower the ground became stonier until we were walking on long slopes of scree. Torches were forbidden; there was no moon and not even much starlight. The mujahideen seemed to be able to see in the dark, but we slipped and stumbled and eventually I fell. Luckily, despite my curses, I did not hurt myself, but a few minutes later Tony came a real cropper behind me. The bushes of camel thorn were almost undetectable, since they were merely a darker blur among other blurs, but, if you trod on one, it threw you off balance. More dangerous was a sudden boulder or invisible drop in the path. As we grew more exhausted we stumbled more frequently, and then Nigel gave a cry and came down like a telephone pole, knocking my legs from under me. As I fell I thought angrily how clumsy he was being. We got up rubbing our knees and elbows. There was nothing for it but to keep going. Gul Bas had disappeared a long time before.

I concentrated furiously on following the path, which was the palest blur of all, but kept hitting my toes on invisible stones. This was painful, tiring and irritating. We walked like this for a couple of hours, slipping and stumbling on the rounded stones until a halt was called on the last hill above the river. Someone pointed out a faint light below us and said that was the bridge. Gul Bas appeared, a shadowy figure.

'There are Russian tanks near the bridge, so don't smoke and don't talk,' Tony translated. I thought this was pretty silly since we had made so much noise sliding and stumbling over the scree that any Russian lookout would surely have heard us already.

As we waited in the slight chill, there was a commotion below us and Gul Bas veered off quickly to one side. Some people had been spotted coming up the hill towards us. They turned out to be local mujahideen who were going to guide us across the river, but in the dark it was easy to see how friend could be mistaken for foe. The anxious moment passed; there were handshakes, a whispered council of war and then below us and to the right, a light started flashing on-off, on-off. We set off again, making a tremendous noise on the scree, slipping and sliding down the last few hundred yards to the river.

I had expected a fair-sized river but it was, mercifully, a complete anti-climax. The Kabul River, which rises in the Hindu Kush and is a hundred yards wide when it joins the Indus at Attock, was only about thirty yards across and a foot or two deep. I forded it with my boots on and without getting my knees wet. There was no sign of any Russian or Afghan troops. The mujahideen crossed in bare feet and stopped a few yards up the hill by an irrigation channel to put their boots on. I emptied mine, wrung out my socks and squelched my way another hundred yards up the hill to wait for the horses. When they arrived only twenty minutes or so later, we discovered that the animal Tom had been riding had to go back to Pakistan and the owner wanted 2,500 Afghanis (£25) in settlement. At midnight it was a typically infuriating development. None of us had any money on us; the expedition's funds were all carefully packed away in a camera box on a horse which had gone on ahead. Finally, Gul Bas had to pay for us, laboriously counting out the Afghanis by the light of a torch, while Jamil and the others argued at the tops of their voices. It occurred to me once again that, had there been any Russians on the bridge or on night patrol, we would have made a very simple target.

After the money had been agreed, the horse and its owner disappeared into the dark, presumably to re-ford the river and climb all the way up that terrible scree again, while we plodded on, longing to reach a village where we could rest. 'How far?' we asked.

'*Nim szad*' (half an hour) came the answer, the inevitable answer as we were to learn. Afghans have no idea of time in the Western sense. They are not bound by planes and trains that allegedly run to the minute and, although all of them now carry watches, I felt that they were worn more as ornaments than as timepieces. So the famous *nim szad* – half an hour's walking time, Afghan speed – we found to be very elastic. You could always safely double it and often double it again. In fact it took us two hours to reach the village where we were going to sleep; two agonizing hours of climbing in the dark, slipping and stumbling.

We arrived around two o'clock, completely exhausted, to find the village deserted, having being bombed by the Russians a month before. Gul Bas indicated a flat piece of ground – it looked like a threshing floor – at the foot of a slope below the houses. We unrolled our sleeping bags in a row, too tired to do anything except lie down and let sleep invade us like a miraculous tide that would sweep away the fatigue of the day.

We were woken at five. Dawn brought a splendid view of the plains below and very empty stomachs. We had had nothing to eat or drink the night before and, the village being empty, there was no breakfast either. The mujahideen wanted us to be on our way by six but we all rebelled, particularly Jean-José. I suppose Gul Bas was terrified in case anything should happen to us, since he would be personally answerable to Masud, and the Russians did start their air war early in the morning. We finally tramped off at seven, the sun already hot and by eight we were parched and very hungry.

Half-way down a hillside, below another empty village, we came on a delicious streamlet and sank down gratefully on the grass. A small boy who was herding goats appeared to examine us and Gul Bas proposed resting until two o'clock when the sun would be less fierce. But with no prospect of food here, we all felt it would be better to push on to the next village where apparently things would be better. It was now intensely hot and we were extremely tired; but we

managed to keep going by a sort of automatic pilot, our feet finding
their own way along the stony path.

At one o'clock, Nigel and I were coming down a narrow, burning
defile when, faintly at first, we heard the sound of water. As we
descended it became steadily louder and eventually unmistakably
the roar of a waterfall. We rounded the corner and there, like some
magic stream from the Arabian Nights, a jet of shining water shot off
the top of a small cliff, fell fifty feet and smashed into thousands of
shimmering diamonds among the rocks at the foot. We hurried
forward and walked right under the waterfall as if it had been a giant
shower bath, letting the cold water thunder over us with a force that
almost took our breath away. Bliss, heaven, delicious coolness. I
stood under it for fifteen or twenty minutes, turning my face up into
the full force of the limpid cascade, washing my hair, face and body
and keeping only my underpants on.

Here, in ultra-Islamic Afghanistan, they consider nudity a sin and
an abomination, so we were denied the ultimate pleasure of standing
under the waterfall as God made us. Indeed when Tony and I
wanted to go back in the evening for another and this time
completely naked wash, we were told that the mullah had already
been complaining about our near-nudity, and the mujahideen said
to flout his wishes would only upset the locals. All the same, we spent
an extremely pleasant and relaxed afternoon, lying in the shade
drinking tea and lunching off rice and yoghurt. Yoghurt seems to
taste better in Afghanistan than anywhere else, perhaps because we
were so hungry, and we gobbled at great speed the bowlfuls that the
villagers brought to us under the trees. These last two days, I wrote
in my diary, were already receding from our minds as exhausting
and almost horrendous experiences. Almost, but not quite!

Later we started filming the mujahideen as they relaxed, cleaned
their weapons and drank tea. They took to the camera without any
real sign of embarrassment. It is always a relief to get the first
pictures 'in the can'. I felt elation now that we had really started and
that the camera equipment had survived the journey so far.

4

Next morning, our sixth day on the march, Charles and Tom left the village early ahead of the convoy, to film it coming up the mountain. I followed later with Gul Bas, and Charles took a good shot of us as we toiled past the camera; I, feeling slightly ridiculous, in my long shirt, baggy trousers and P.L.O. scarf, and trying not to look too nonchalant. After all, it was bloody hard work! The shots of the convoy turned out extremely well, giving a good idea of the arms we were carrying: boosters for the RPGs, Chinese plastic mines shaped rather like a summer pudding, and tin boxes of ammunition, the whole thing given an unexpectedly pastoral quality by the musical tinkle of the donkey bells.

It was only after we had finished filming that I realized we had let the camera horse go past. It was already three or four hundred yards away across the mountain and I ran after it, discarding my pack, my boots pounding along the stony path, dodging past the intervening donkeys and horses. Eventually, about three-quarters of a mile further on, I caught up with the horse and driver and, angry and out of breath, shouted and gesticulated at him to go back. He either misunderstood or, more likely, did not like being shouted at by a foreigner and an infidel, and stubbornly refused to turn round. We waited beside the path in mute hostility until Gul Bas came trudging by and told the driver to wait for Charles. A few minutes later Nigel came racing up the path with the heavy recorder over his shoulder, explaining that Tom and Charles had had a row and were not speaking to one another. Then Charles arrived, panting, and after some muttering and black looks, the camera was loaded. The driver, still stony-faced, accepted a toffee as a peace offering.

We slogged on across the parched mountainscape, our eyes longing for a patch of green until, at around half-past twelve, we came to an inhabited village and collapsed gratefully in the shade of some huge mulberry trees by a stream. Some enchanting children gathered round to stare, the boys demonstrating their uncanny skill with their catapults. Gul Bas negotiated refreshments and, after twenty minutes or so, a cloth was spread on the ground and a large pot of tea and a big plate of home-baked biscuits arrived from the nearest house. It was cool in the shade and utterly peaceful, the stream gurgling gently below us. We took off our boots and aired our blistered feet.

But Gul Bas did not linger long. Half an hour later he led us to the other end of the village and there, to my surprise, called another halt and announced that we would have lunch. I thought it odd that we had not come here in the first place, but such churlish thoughts were rapidly driven away by the warmth of our host's welcome. A carpet was spread beneath a tree on the edge of a field of maize, cushions were brought for our heads and, after half an hour of delicious indolence, a tomato omelette swimming in oil arrived, accompanied by hot freshly baked *nan*. Eating communally tends to bring out the worst in one, I find, since the fastest and greediest eaters come off best. The omelette disappeared in no time and we lay back with full stomachs to sip our green tea. I wrote in my diary that night: 'All in all, the best meal so far.' A week's privation had reduced my horizons to those of a schoolboy: food had become all-important.

We set off again when the sun was lower and walked for a couple of hours to the village where we were to spend the night. We caught sight first of the vineyards, a cool green splash in the harsh brown landscape and, beyond them, a cluster of mud-walled houses, looking, as do all Pathan villages, like desert forts, their walls high and thick enough to repel invaders. The centre of the village was shaded by enormous mulberry trees overhanging a muddy pool where children were splashing happily.

We were installed in the mosque, often the only lodging available in these villages. The walls were decorated with simple childish drawings, some of which were of tanks and planes, depicting the war. Normal life was represented by pictures of Bedford lorries, which are still popular in this part of the world, their owners decorating them lavishly and garishly. There was straw on the floor and it was clean and airy, but, for some reason that was not immediately clear, the mullah had us moved to the house of the headman. He turned out to be extremely bossy, shouting and pushing at anyone who did not jump to his command. Maybe he was upset at being saddled with us, and he muttered angrily when I squirted my anti-flea powder on the part of the floor and wall which I guessed would be the bridgehead for the customary night attack.

Supper came eventually, first the greasy soup, then, congealing on a separate plate, bits of boiled goat or mutton which our obliging fellow diners shredded on to the inevitable rice. If one was quick one might get a tasty morsel, otherwise one was liable to end up with a cold bit of bone and gristle. With it came the equally inevitable *nan* and the always welcome tea: either *sabs*, green tea, which I found more refreshing, or *sia*, black tea, which is stronger and which most Afghans prefer. Exhausted, I climbed into my sleeping bag immediately afterwards, despite the curious stares of our host and his friends, and was quickly asleep.

At 8.30 next morning, we had tea and *nan* in the mosque, first edging past the faithful to find a space on the floor. Later we heard a loud bang and then the sound of a jet. A bomb, I thought, or more likely, the sonic boom of a jet breaking the sound barrier. I wanted to get some shots of the village, so we climbed up a steep hill opposite. As we arrived at the top we heard the beat of a MI-24 helicopter gunship. It was so high as to pose no real danger but, even so, people in the village below us ran for cover.

The light was so brilliant that everything stood out with a clarity that was almost breathtaking, reminding me of the light in Greece; the light that gave us the work of Praxiteles, the splendour of the Parthenon. Here there was nothing like that, no art, no human vision on that scale; the landscape was the masterpiece.

We climbed down to find the drivers and the mujahideen cooking their own lunch, but no provision seemed to have been made for us. So Nigel, as soupmaster, decided we would broach some of Mr Knorr's packets, and the rest of us were detailed to collect wood and start a fire. The only available spot was near the communal lavatory and there was no shade. The sun was now near its zenith and blazingly hot. As we squatted round the fire, puffing and blowing, we were roasted on two sides at once. Passers-by found this funny but only the village idiot offered to help and we shooed him away. The soup took a long time to cook, needing to be brought to the boil first and then simmered for fifteen minutes. Nigel was very much in charge, spoon in hand and looking like a lean and rather demented chef. We had just gulped down a few burning hot mouthfuls when Agha Gul, piratical as ever, arrived with rice and *nan*. Lunch *à l'Afghan* was then prepared and, after haranguing the mujahideen with great force, Agha Gul departed to rejoin his half of the convoy which was bringing up the rear. He certainly was a dynamic customer and obviously important: these convoys were the only supply lines available to Masud and his men.

We left the village at 4.30 and climbed for a steady hour to reach a crest from which we looked down on the great plain of Shomali, stretching away into the distance. The mujahideen pointed out Bagram airbase, shimmering like a salt pan about ten miles away on the left. I could just make out the gleam of the runways, but the sound of the jets taking off and landing was quite clear in the still desert air. The mujahideen also pointed out another landmark: the great wall of the Hindu Kush rising in a blue barrier at the far end of the plain and just visible through the haze. Beyond that, we knew, lay our destination, the Panjsher Valley, Masud's stronghold and the symbol of Afghan Resistance. It was an emotional moment. We still had a long way to go, but at last we were within sight of our objective.

We descended the hill, stopping for a rest on a bright green patch of grass beside a stream. Tony and Jean-José got out their cameras and took a picture of all of us; the muj looking serious and clasping their weapons in the stiff pose they always adopted when they saw a camera. Another MIG roared off the distant runway into the cloudless blue sky as a group of donkeys, their bells tinkling, came neat-footed down the path with their loads of green RPG rocket boosters. We made haste down the hillside just in case the Russians had a lookout with binoculars trained on the path, and then started off across the Koh-i-Safi Desert at the foot of the mountain, walking in what turned out to be a huge semi-circle to avoid Bagram. Any low-flying helicopter would have spotted the long line of men and animals but none appeared – perhaps they did not expect a mujahideen convoy to pass so close to the base. Feeling safer with darkness, we plodded on across the plain, glad for once to be able to walk on the flat. We went through several villages without stopping, the dogs barking ferociously, and I got the impression that the villagers were not particularly keen to know us.

This night march was less terrible than the crossing of the Kabul
River: at least there was some moon and the ground was less stony.
Even so we stumbled and tripped in the dark. Ahead of us green and
white flares described lazy parabolas in the dark sky. When we
stopped for a rest in one big village Gul Bas gave orders for no
smoking and no torches. We could see the glow of Bagram's lights
clearly now and once we were clear of the village the airbase came
into view. Even at a distance of three or four miles we could see the
perimeter fence was brilliantly floodlit, and flares rose constantly
into the sky. As one flare blossomed and then slowly parachuted
towards the ground, another would rocket silently, burst and float
down, so that there was always one in the sky. The Russians must be
windy, I thought, and I remembered Masud's claim that I had heard
in Paris, that in a raid on Bagram in May, his men had destroyed
several helicopters and jets on the ground.

We walked for several hours but Bagram seemed to be always on
our left, more or less in the same position. Perhaps it was further
away than we thought. We crossed one small river and then finally,
after a long march, we came to the Panjsher River, which after
leaving the Panjsher Valley turns south-east to join the Kabul River.
Some say that Panjsher means Five Tigers and certainly the river
here has five arms, all fairly shallow in summer but fast-running.

We debated among ourselves whether to cross barefoot or in boots
– I decided to keep my boots on – but a more important debate was
going on among the mujahideen: they seemed to be lost. We milled
about indecisively on the bank of the river while our escorts argued
loudly among themselves. Finally, fed up with what might be a
dangerous delay, we followed a couple of mujahideen into the cold
water and waded to the far bank. We repeated this five times, the last
crossing being the most difficult, the water very fast-running, thigh
deep and the rocks very slippery. The speed of the water had the
effect of making me lose my balance and I began to stagger about.
Gul Bas, who was watching impatiently from the far side, came
wading out to help me, grabbing me by the arm and steering me to
the bank. The others came splashing behind, in bare feet and
carrying their boots. As soon as we reached the bank, Gul Bas urged
us on.

'He says hurry up, there are Russians on the top of the hill,' Tony
translated. I needed to empty the water out of my boots and Charles
and the others wanted to dry their feet and put their boots on, so

another ten minutes went by with Gul Bas becoming more and more agitated. It was around midnight when we were finally ready to clump off into the darkness, the lights of Bagram still blazing in the distance. We had been walking for nearly eight hours already and there was still a long way to go.

We now entered a belt of loess, top-soil dust, as fine as powder and about six inches deep. It was like walking in cotton wool and, although the night was perfectly still, clouds of choking dust rose and hung in the air. Being near the tail of the convoy, we could not escape it. It got into everything, ears, nostrils, mouth, hair and eyes, and covered everyone with a pale grey coating, like a sugared fruit. When we eventually stopped for a rest, I thought I would never be able to get up again.

At 3.30, with the dim mass of the Hindu Kush rising out of the plain ahead of us, we stumbled into a village called Karazak, just below the mountain. We were so exhausted that we went to sleep with our boots on, just outside the mosque. What exquisite pleasure it was merely to lie down, despite the hardness of the ground.

I woke with a hangover from sheer fatigue, covered in dust and with a mouth like the bottom of the proverbial parrot's cage. I managed to lever myself into a sitting position to drink tea, and slowly came to as the sun rose and warmed us. After breakfast we crossed the dried-up river to the far side of the village, climbed an orchard wall and came to a sort of terrace overhung by a beautiful old vine, very gnarled and twisted, and bereft, alas, of grapes. The owner spread a couple of carpets on the bone-dry soil and brought tea and dried mulberries, and we lay there looking down the valley towards Kabul, hidden behind pale purple mountains. We went back to the mosque for a lunch of delicious stewed aubergines and admired the paintings on the wall of Russian jets being shot down by mujahideen with AK47s, a piece of absurd optimism which I found touching and very typical of the Afghan character. The old mullah, a small saintly figure with an impressive beard, sat on a bed in the corner, wrapped in his own thoughts.

After lunch we washed in the stream and rested, comforted by the information that tonight's march would be a short one. We were now north-east of Bagram – we could hear the constant sound of jets and helicopters in the distance – and just south of Gulbahar, near the mouth of the Panjsher Valley, looking down on a flat green plain, with the imposing bulk of the Hindu Kush looming behind us.

The short march turned out to be a six-hour slog. Cursing, we slipped and stumbled over rocks in the dark, following stream beds for much of the way, passing through a series of villages and finally climbing right up the mountainside to a remote house, where we staggered on to the flat roof and collapsed. We were angry with Gul Bas for his infuriating habit of telling us that our destination was only half an hour away when in reality it was two more hours distant.

Tony was so cross that he rounded on him, declaring: 'I expect Communists to tell us lies, not the mujahideen.'

Our irritation was sharpened by the absence of any sustenance on arrival – not even a cup of tea. We had to content ourselves with a glass of water before unrolling our sleeping bags and crawling into them. For a moment or two, I lay on my back gazing up at the stars, something that one does all too rarely. The night was warm and velvety; perhaps because of the unsullied nature of the Afghan atmosphere the sky looked blacker and the stars larger and brighter than in Europe. The fatigue and irritation of the day dropped away and I lay there, a swimmer suspended in a motionless sea, as sleep came with god-like swiftness.

We were up at five and by half-past were trudging up the mountain. It was spectacularly beautiful, huge rocks and slabs of granite littering the hillside. Somehow, with amazing resource and energy, the locals have managed to terrace and irrigate this inhospitable terrain, growing mulberries and walnuts in abundance. At six, Russian jets started to overfly us, heading in the direction, I presumed, of the Panjsher Valley. I noted in my diary: 'I breakfasted off mulberries and relieved myself in a cleft of the mountain, serenaded by MIGs. Two bomb bursts some distance away.'

By mid-morning we reached the little village of Boularenn, clinging to a steep hillside above the river. We camped out on what looked like a threshing floor, a small sweep of dried, packed earth half-way between the houses and the river, shaded by a huge mulberry tree. The local headman, small, friendly and talkative, a sort of Afghan Ulysses, spread carpets for our comfort and brought tea to slake our thirst. Later, we scrambled down to the river to paddle our feet in the cold clear water and doctor our blisters. Jean-Philippe had advised us that if they were just beginning we should tape them up tightly, but if they were large, then it was better to burst them and apply some ferocious-looking red ointment, of which he seemed to have an inexhaustible supply.

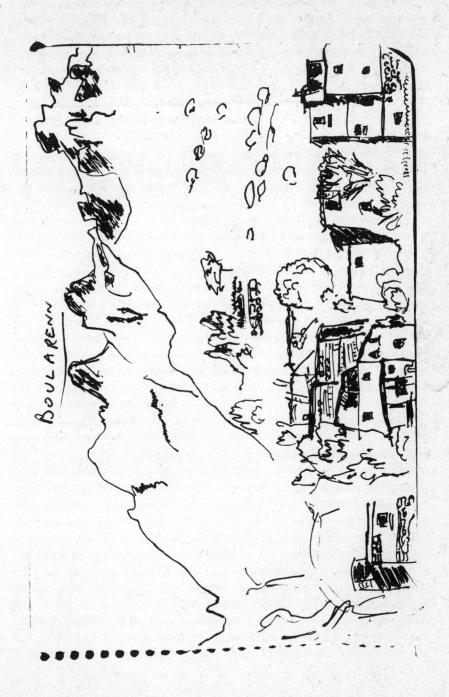

We were going to spend the rest of the day and the night here, so in self-indulgent mood, I got out my diary and tried to sketch some of the higgledy-piggledy houses above the river. They were all different, clinging to the hillside and one another like swallows' nests, and yet with an air of considerable solidity. These village houses have virtually no amenities, no running water, no electricity and very few have inside lavatories – or lavatories of any kind, come to that. One imagines they have not changed their style for hundreds and possibly thousands of years. Their inhabitants may be backward in some ways but they are hugely hospitable and independent. Every man has a weapon, often an old British Lee Enfield 303, stamped with a crown and dated around 1860, although many have more up-to-date weapons too.

I was summoned from my sketching by a shout that lunch was about to be served and I climbed up the hill to find that Ulysses had prepared quite a spread. A relay of Ulysses' relatives brought bowls of soup, plates of boiled mutton (what a relief not to have goat!), potatoes, spring onions and, for dessert, grapes; succulent green, shiny grapes. For once reasonably replete, we spent the afternoon lolling in the shade, reading and sleeping. We had brought a fair selection of paperbacks with us, notably *Kim*, *Vanity Fair* and several books about Afghanistan, although the classic work by Dupree was so heavy, even in paperback, that it had been relegated to the heavy luggage. At five, the jets again started howling across the sky with the regularity of tube trains, on their way to bomb the Panjsher.

Something now happened which was destined to be a turning point in our expedition and very nearly a disastrous one. All along, we had imagined that our pack-train would deliver us and our equipment safely to the Panjsher at the end of the journey. But now, Tony, translating for Gul Bas, announced some startling news. The horses and donkeys were stopping here, at Boularenn, and all the arms and our equipment would be unloaded and stored until they could be brought in by porters later. The explanation was that, because of the bombing, we would have to make a detour next day over a twelve-thousand-foot pass, which was too steep for the animals. I suspect this was an excuse and that really the drivers refused to go any further because of the risk of being caught in the open and strafed by the Russians. Or maybe Gul Bas thought it was too risky. At any rate our immediate reaction was to say no, we could not be separated from our equipment. A long argument developed, interrupted at one point by an invitation from Gul Bas to go and see how safe our equipment would be.

Charles and I climbed up the steep path to a house built against the rock face. In a storeroom at the bottom, most of the arms and all our equipment had been dumped in a complete muddle. As we sorted through it, looking for our own stuff, Ulysses became excited by a buzzing noise coming from Nigel's kitbag.

'What's that?' he asked excitedly, 'A bomb?' I opened the kitbag, mystified myself, until I realized it was his electric razor which had somehow been switched on and was humming away like an angry bee. I finally extracted it, held it aloft and switched it off to general applause. Then I noticed that my *pattu*, which had been strapped across the top of my rucksack, was missing. I told Gul Bas who looked upset but could do nothing about it. The drivers had gone back with the horses and one of them, presumably, was the richer by my *pattu*.

We returned to the mulberry tree, where Ulysses and his family were preparing the evening meal. While they lit the oil lamps and spread a long cloth on the carpets, we debated the crisis. We all knew the golden rule: that you should never be separated from your camera equipment. Unfortunately television equipment is heavy, whether video or film, too heavy for even quite fit Westerners like us to porter over a twelve-thousand-foot mountain. We knew we could not carry it ourselves. I asked Gul Bas, via Tony, whether we could not get porters to carry in at least the camera and one or two other vital pieces. Gul Bas shook his head. The truth was that the mujahideen did not like portering and Gul Bas did not seem to have the authority to recruit local villagers. I blamed myself afterwards that we did not at this stage break down the equipment into a basic operating unit consisting of the camera, a recorder and a rucksack for tapes and spare batteries. But even then we would have needed three porters and they just did not seem to be available.

Forced to change his plan because of the bombing, Gul Bas argued that we should press on to the Panjsher where Masud would make all the necessary arrangements.

'He says that once we see Masud, there will be no problem. Masud will give orders to have the stuff brought in.'

'How long will it take, though?' we wanted to know.

'A few days only,' came the answer and with that we had to be content.

One alternative had occurred to me. We could split up, two of us going on to see Masud, while the other two waited behind with the equipment. It was tempting in one way, but on balance I thought it better for the team to stay together, although separated from the equipment. As soon as we reached Masud I would impress on him, with all the force at my command, the urgent need to bring in the equipment. In any case, as a final argument, I concluded that since Masud needed his arms just as much as we needed our equipment, there would be as little delay as possible. I went to sleep under the stars, with the roar of the river in my ears, slightly unhappy at the thought of leaving all the equipment behind, but too tired to argue further. We had now been on the march for nine days and physical exhaustion was taking its toll.

5

Next morning at 7.15 we started 'the last great march to the Panjsher', as we thought; a long hard thirsty climb up through magnificent rocks and granite cliffs, reaching the first pass around noon. In front of us lay the most tremendous view of the Panjsher, running north-east to south-west, two great walls of mountains rising above the narrow valley. Everywhere we looked, other ranges rose one after the other to the horizon. At two we reached another col, from which we had an equally superb view. Snow was still lying in some of the high corries on the far side of the valley and, beyond, a sea of peaks stretched into the distance.

On our way down we passed the first refugees living in stone lean-tos among the rocks. One man had been wounded by a bomb splinter and Jean-Philippe crossed the river to attend to him. We had heard the explosion on our way down and Charles had tried to film, with a small Autoload film camera, the puff of smoke where the bomb landed. Shortly afterwards, when he was trying to get a shot of a jet flying high overhead, the spring on the Autoload broke, robbing us of our last chance of taking moving pictures.

We were getting used to the sound of Russian jets now. For most of the day they howled across the sky high above us, although we heard no more explosions; no doubt they were busy further up the valley. We climbed all the way down to the bottom of a side valley, but when we realized that Gul Bas intended to climb all the way up the far side, we went on strike. It was five, the light was going and it seemed more sensible to make camp where we were rather than blunder about on the mountainside in the dark. Gul Bas tried to cajole us, saying that there was a house further on where we could spend the night. All I could see, as I peered up the precipitous valley ahead, was a great jumble of rocks, some as big as houses. When Gul Bas saw that we were determined, he and his companions retired in a sulk.

Nigel and I had brought some packets of soup in our small rucksacks and now we all started to gather firewood. It was a wild and lonely spot, with a stream cascading over a great rib of rock and a few goat and sheep shelters, made of dry stone, nearby. There was not much wood but we collected everything that would burn, bits of camel thorn and hemlock and cattle droppings, and somehow got a fire started. When the sun went down it became chilly and we huddled round the pitiful little fire for warmth. It took almost an hour to make the soup, which was lumpy but hot and warmed us up. We would have gone hungry to bed but luckily Gul Bas had relented and, just as I was climbing into my sleeping bag which I had unrolled in a sheep shelter, he reappeared with some villagers carrying a pot of rice and a few lumps of boiled goat. We made our peace round the embers of the fire. I wrote in my diary: 'I get the impression that the continuing Russian pressure is disturbing Panjsher life pretty considerably.'

We suffered ourselves next day by having to make a long and very steep detour up a side valley. We were moving parallel to the main valley and having to climb up and down over subsidiary ridges. A four-engined Russian reconnaissance plane, an Antonov, droned overhead. When we reached the next crest I turned and looked back at the col we had crossed the day before. It looked a very long way away and I traced with my eye how we had gone right down almost to the level of the floor of the main valley and then come half-way up again. It seemed a waste of effort. We now started a long traverse along the side of the mountain, out boots slipping on the fine scree. Each time I skidded I tried to stop myself by grabbing a bush, (until I learned that they were all prickly) either camel thorn, with long spikes that can inflict a nasty gash, or dog roses which scratch like a wild cat. Wheatears and redstarts, flirting their fiery orange rumps, flew from stone to stone beside us, chiding us with their staccato cries. Down below, somewhere near Rokha, the main town in the valley which we knew was occupied by the Russians, we could hear the intermittent thump of a heavy mortar. Crump . . . crump. . . .

As we goat-scrambled along one particularly exposed hillside, there came the beat of MI-24 helicopters. Gul Bas waved at us to get down. I lay beside the path, feeling very exposed, having lost my protective *pattu* which was intended precisely for emergencies like these. A few minutes later the helicopters started to rocket and bomb the valley floor. The rockets made a wicked crack as they were fired, followed by a streak of smoke and then a sharp report and puffs of smoke as they struck home. The helicopters circled, their flight somehow all the more frightening for being so slow and deliberate, and unleashed a pair of bombs, throwing up clouds of dust and smoke. The explosions reverberated off the sides of the valley. One helicopter turned away and blasted the face of the mountain, presumably aiming for a mujahideen machine gun placed somewhere high up. The jets came over again, like little express trains in the sky, small silver shapes hurtling across the blue, towing their siren of death.

When they had gone we dropped down to the floor of the side valley where the going was easier, but soon turned off up another side valley. We climbed past a number of refugee families living among the rocks before stopping at one lean-to. A solid stone wall had been built to meet the rock overhang. There was a narrow doorway at the far end and we entered to find a cool, shady interior. We were made to sit down on carpets, cushions were thrust behind our backs and the host, a lean, middle-aged Afghan in Western trousers and a smart, blue-striped shirt which reminded me of Turnbull & Asser's in Jermyn Street, came forward to shake hands. He said he had been a bus driver in Kabul before the Russian invasion, but now, as a Panjsheri, he had come home to join the Resistance. He was a good-looking man, almost distinguished, more like a diplomat than a bus driver.

As we reclined on our cushions, drinking tea, there was a commotion outside and a personage of some note strode in. This splendid-looking gentleman with a luxuriant beard promptly embraced us, kissing us each on the cheek three times. This was the first time we had received the traditional Afghan greeting and I felt we had really been accepted into the ranks of the Resistance. Our visitor was the local Commander who had heard of our arrival and had come to thank us for coming to the Panjsher. Rice was brought and more tea and it was not until after three that Gul Bas said we must proceed.

Tom, now deprived of his horse, was having trouble with his legs and said he could go no further without a rest. We decided he should stay the night with the hospitable bus driver and Charles for company, while Nigel and I pressed on so as to reach Masud as soon as possible. It was just as well. The climb up was relentless and just about all I could manage, although only carrying a light rucksack. Several times Jean-Philippe, with a generosity that I found touching, offered to carry it for me. Since he was carrying nothing, I let him do so, although to my shame Nigel toiled up unaided carrying his rucksack.

It took us about four hours to reach the top, by which time the mountains behind us were lost in a purple haze, while in front of us they stood out green and brown in the last rays of the sun. By the time we were half-way down the far side it was completely dark and we found it more and more difficult to negotiate the rocky path. After one or two falls that could easily have ended in a twisted ankle, Tony, Nigel and I all decided that we had had enough. We would unroll our sleeping bags and spend the night on the hillside. Tony shouted the news down to Gul Bas who became so agitated that he turned and strode up the hill towards us. As he drew level, furious that we should countermand his orders, Tony said we had decided to stay where we were. Gul Bas exploded, screaming out at the top of his voice in Farsi and hurling his torch on the ground. Miraculously it continued to work. I was watering Afghanistan at the time, my back towards them and merely commented, 'Silly bloody man.'

A long altercation followed, with poor Tony taking the brunt of it, and then Gul Bas stumped off furiously.

The wretched man seemed to have no savvy. He must have known it would take four hours to reach the top and that we would be caught on the mountain in the dark. So why did he allow us to stay so long in the bus driver's cave? It was this inability of the Afghans to get their timing right that was so infuriating, we told one another. As a result of Gul Bas's incompetence we risked breaking a leg in the dark, and if that should happen, and it would have been quite easy, our expedition would have been finished. And that would have been a misfortune for the Afghans as well as for ourselves.

But now Jean-José and Jean-Philippe, who had remained below, called up encouragingly. The route was easier, they said, and it was apparently not too far to the next village, where we would spend the night in far greater comfort than up here on the bare mountain. After some discussion, very reasonable now after the flare of anger, we agreed to go on. It was a long and exhausting hike down and we did not reach the outskirts of Abdullah Kheil until almost midnight. Even then we had to walk for about another half-mile, skirting the walls of enormously tall houses built on outcrops of rock, following the irrigation channel that ran through the village, and ducking under the trunk of a giant mulberry or walnut tree growing between two houses at an angle of forty-five degrees.

At last, exhausted, we stopped outside a doorway. There followed a long wait while the master of the house was roused. He eventually appeared, lantern in hand, and led us past the odd sheep in the hall to an upstairs room where a handful of men were already stretched out on the carpet. One man was sleeping on a small balcony outside the window and he put his head up and stared at me in surprise as I went through my sleeping-bag ritual. Afghans simply wrap themselves in any available quilt or blanket and stretch out fully clothed on the floor. Getting up is equally simple. They therefore watched in amazement as we unrolled our lightweight sleeping bags and undressed inside them. This had to be done surreptitiously as, even in a room with only men present, it was considered indecent to expose any part of the flesh. Charles kept getting into trouble for standing up bare-legged in the morning and drawing on his trousers beneath the startled gaze of our Afghan hosts.

Word would be passed to Tony, who would then have to say to Charles: 'For God's sake, Charles, don't walk about without your trousers on; they get very upset.'

One trick, however, never failed to captivate the audience. This was what Nigel called the daily miracle of putting the genie back in its bottle. These down sleeping bags, quite bulky when spread out, rolled up so neatly that they fitted into a nylon bag that was not much bigger than a bottle, or at any rate a magnum. It really was a remarkable feat of compression that never ceased to amaze me, let alone the Afghans.

In my budget for the trip I had estimated a week to ten days maximum to reach the Panjsher and yet here we were on the morning of the twelfth day, still a day's march away. I was also becoming alarmed about our separation from the equipment which Gul Bas was now saying would take perhaps five or six days to reach us and by the savage difficulty of the terrain. Filming here was clearly going to be the most arduous thing we had ever done.

Still, it was a lovely morning and after a wash in the irrigation channel below the house, watched by two women and several small boys, and breakfast of tea and *nan*, my spirits began to rise. As we set off along the banks of the irrigation channel, the water running fast and clear between tall blue daisies, the beauty of the Darra Valley unfolded before our eyes. Fields of ripening wheat and maize, neatly terraced between high stone walls, fell away to the river on our right. Big, solid, mud and timber houses, some with a stone foundation, were dotted about the smiling valley, some like miniature castles, their flat roofs already laden with rounded stacks of hay and winter fodder. When we came to a group of heavily-laden apricot trees, the mujahideen climbed up and shook the boughs, bringing down a golden rain of apricots. They were sweet and juicy, and the old men and women to whom they presumably belonged smiled and told us to help ourselves. We were, of course, on home territory here and there was none of the animosity we had sensed in the south. The house beyond the apricots had a new ladder resting against the wall. It was a solid tree trunk, with the steps cut out like a staircase. Simple and practical.

We marched on down the valley. This is what I imagined the whole of the Panjsher must have been like before the war: serene, rich, peaceful. The whole valley was terraced, irrigated, carefully husbanded. We had heard a bang at breakfast time and now someone said that a man working in the fields had been killed by an anti-personnel mine. These are small plastic mines usually dropped by helicopter and powerful enough to blow off the hand or foot of anyone who picks up or steps on one. We heard some jets go over very high.

After two or three hours we came to a tributary of the main river, which we crossed by a flimsy bridge. Below us the water made an invitingly deep, green pool. A little further on, across a litter of rocks, we came on a big meadow shaded by trees and stopped to rest. The locals gave us no lunch except a great basketful of fresh mulberries, newly shaken from the trees and washed in the river. We fell on them with a voracious appetite and ate and ate until I, at any rate, felt slightly sick. We crossed the river and carried on down towards the main valley, passing more deep green pools which I longed to dive into. Boys were splashing about in them but no adults. Despite assurances that things were much freer and easier in the Panjsher, I began to wonder.

Gul Bas, scenting home, kept the pace up, and there were effusive greetings from acquaintances every few hundred yards. Around four, we ran into the two lieutenants from the convoy, who lived in a farm fifty yards from the road and who invited us in for tea. On the far side of a harvested wheatfield, carpets were spread in the shade of a huge mulberry tree. We sank down wearily while the brothers arranged cushions and made us comfortable. Tea was brought and I realized that my stomach felt very empty: we had eaten nothing of substance all day. It was pleasant here, lounging in the shade, and doubly satisfying to know that at last we had arrived. It was Sunday, 22 August, twelve days after leaving the Pakistan border. One of the brothers said Masud was coming to meet us and was expected either that evening or next morning. Our spirits immediately rose. Once we could talk to him and explain the difficulties about our equipment, our problems would be over. Or so I fondly imagined. Other friends and members of the family arrived to drink tea and talk and then, as the light failed, they all went off to pray, leaving the five of us (Tony, Jean-José, Jean-Philippe, Nigel and myself) to attend to our *toilette* and our blisters.

After prayers, oil lamps were brought and then supper; an exquisite tomato and onion salad, boiled rice and grapes. Afterwards, over tea, we had a long account from the brothers of how the Russians, and they said East Germans as well, had attacked the Darra Valley and their village of Tambonnah, at the beginning of July. Tanks had advanced up the dry river bed and helicopters had ferried troops on to the high ground. The Russians had made eight separate attacks in forty days, burning and destroying a large number of houses. According to Jean-José, Masud's master plan was always to try to hold the main valley as far as the confluence at Do Ab (Two Rivers) and the Darra Valley (where we were), since it was the richest of the side valleys and the main route to Pakistan.

The brothers came from a large family and its fortunes seemed to mirror the plight of the whole country. One brother was still in Kabul, where he worked, surprisingly, in the Ministry of Defence, one was in America and one in Germany, while our two friends ran the farm as well as being active in the Resistance. They were young, about twenty or twenty-one and full of hatred and contempt for the Russians.

'We will fight the Russians for a hundred years, if we have to,' one of them said, summing up their mood of youthful defiance.

Around ten, with the night becoming cool and windy, and no sign of Masud, we made ready for bed; to sleep where we had dined, under the mulberry tree beneath the stars, with the sound of the river in our ears.

Next morning, at 7.30, as we sat waiting for our tea, there was a stir in the trees behind us, downriver, and I turned to see a small group of men approaching in single file. The one in front looked young and vigorous, with the quality of leadership about him and I thought: Masud. This is him. At last. I wondered if he would measure up to our expectations, which had been magnified, I suppose, by distance and our arduous trek. He wore a khaki combat jacket, khaki trousers, black Russian army boots, chequered scarf and a flat woollen, Chitrali cap. As he came nearer I saw that he was pale-skinned, with a wispy beard, about medium height and that he walked with the smallest of stoops. Then he was among us and everyone was standing almost at attention, as deferential as Afghans can ever be, and I was aware of an aura, a mystique that seemed to set him apart. As I shook his hand I noticed above all his eyes, quick and intelligent. He had a long, slightly Jewish nose and the face of a thinker, perhaps, more than of a man of action. But he had an air of maturity and authority remarkable in a man of only twenty-eight.

We were all about to sit down when a jet whined ominously overhead and immediately Masud and his entourage walked towards the house, with the brothers signing to us to follow. We all crowded into a high-ceilinged, carpeted room and sat round the walls in a big circle. Tea was brought and hot, oiled *nan*. It was the first time we had had this and it was very good. They brought Masud a small tray with a cup and separate pot of milk tea, which is served already mixed and is considered something of a delicacy. We also had it that day, thanks to Masud's presence. Sitting cross-legged in the corner, sipping his tea, Masud rapidly read a sheaf of letters and messages and equally swiftly wrote replies. Afterwards, as he talked to the brothers and other locals, he struck me as being a good listener. I guessed that this was how he received the bulk of his information – by letter and word of mouth. At the end of each conversation he would say a few decisive words, as if he were passing on his instructions.

As I sat watching Masud and his mujahideen, squatting on the dusty carpets in this big, cheerless room with its rough, barrel-vaulted ceiling and dirty whitewashed walls adorned with postcards of Mecca, I thought: this is how Tito and his Partisans must have looked in the 1940s. But was Masud another Tito? It was too early yet to say, but he had a tautness about him and an integrity that was impressive. He looked an honest as well as an intelligent man.

After he had dealt with immediate business, Masud was ready to talk to us. We were taken to a smaller room, unfurnished except for a carpet and cushions. A few minutes later Masud came in alone and sat down. First he spoke to Jean-José, whom he knew from the previous summer, smiling and friendly. Then he turned to us. Nigel had urged me to make as strong a case as possible, since we were not sure how well Masud had been briefed about us and it was vital to get prompt action on the equipment.

I took a deep breath and launched into my carefully rehearsed speech.

'Commander Masud,' I began in French. 'We have come to make a major one-hour documentary for British Independent Television on the Resistance in the Panjsher and on you as its leader. It's a big-budget documentary; it will take three months to make and will be shown to millions of people in Britain, and we hope throughout the world. We would like to film the mujahideen in action and record a long interview with you in Farsi, so that you can express yourself as freely as possible.'

Masud listened attentively, nodding from time to time. Then I explained about the equipment.

'It's absolutely vital that it should be brought in as soon as possible and because it's so heavy, it would be a great help if we could have some transport, if that's possible?'

To my surprise, Masud nodded and said: 'No problem.'

But when I said we would like to follow him around for several days filming him, he replied: 'That would be difficult because I move all the time and it would not be easy for you to keep up.' But he said it in such a way that I felt we would be able to get more or less what we wanted. As to the equipment, he had already given orders for it to be brought in.

Masud then talked about the military situation. There were twelve thousand Russian and Afghan troops in Rokha, he claimed, and, despite the minefields round their positions, he could easily have driven them out, but for one thing. He leaned forward to give emphasis to his words. 'I have information from a very sure source in Kabul that the Russians are going to launch a major ground attack within a week.'

Although we had heard rumours of another possible offensive, Masud's words came as a shock. I felt excited by the thought of what we might get on camera, but apprehensive about being on the receiving end of a Russian offensive.

'Because of this we have to conserve our ammunition. So we are not going to attack Rokha now. We've also heard that the Russians are sending in twelve hundred more men as reinforcements to Rokha, but the mujahideen near Kabul have sent us messages saying they will not let them pass.'

We asked him about the Russian dispositions at Rokha. 'The Government positions are always the same. First, they have mines, then Afghan troops, then Russians behind, to stop the Afghans running away. Without the Russians behind them, the Afghan Army wouldn't fight.'

Just as we were finishing our conversation, the door opened and Charles and Tom burst into the room, sweating from their long walk but triumphant to have found us. They had spent the night in a *qarârgâh* (army headquarters) about half-way down the valley. Masud departed shortly afterwards and we spent most of the day sitting, resting and drinking tea in the big cheerless room. I would have preferred to be out of doors, but our hosts seemed to be anxious to keep us in, whether for our safety or because our presence outside inhibited their women, we could not be sure. Whatever the reason, we all felt a certain constraint.

However we were all outside, watching the light fade on the mountains when around seven o'clock Masud and his party returned, just in time for prayers. Spreading their *pattus* in two lines, they knelt in the stubble of the wheatfield, their weapons beside them, and went through the simple ritual of evening prayer, led by a young mullah, who looked like another mujahid. There were about twenty of them, all young apart from two, one a big barrel-chested sergeant-major figure, the other smaller and rather dour, with a startling resemblance to Asterix the Gaul in the French cartoon. They made a moving and impressive sight, bowing their foreheads to the ground in unison, the purple mountains behind, the air cool, the river loud in the background.

After prayers, we ate by lamplight at the edge of the field, on carpets brought out from the house. At the end of the meal, Masud read and wrote letters, his aquiline profile sharply-drawn in the lamplight, and then talked at length to one man. Sitting slightly to

Nigel Ryan, Tom Murphy and me on the Khyber Pass, August 1982, just before the start of our trek to the Panjsher Valley to find the Afghan Resistance leader, Masud (above)

Terrimangal, on the Pakistan-Afghanistan border, one of the starting points for the guerrilla arms convoys. Here, all the expedition's camera equipment was weighed and then divided up into loads for the pack animals (below)

A rest for a cup of tea after a hard march in from the border. The temperature was in the 80s (above)

Looking down on Bagram, the big Soviet airbase north-east of Kabul, which the convoy skirted at night (centre)

Jean-José Puig, our expert from France, who, with his luxuriant beard and dark looks, could have passed for an Afghan (below)

The Panjsher Valley, the historic route through the Hindu Kush, now Masud's stronghold and a symbol of the Resistance (right)

Mujahideen breaking their journey in a mosque. Most of them are equipped with new Russian-made AK47 automatic rifles (inset)

Harvesting in the Panjsher Valley: the small stony fields are typical. So is the idyllic sense of remoteness

Masud, the best-known guerrilla leader in Afghanistan. He has survived at least six major offensives by the Russians (left)

Masud and mujahideen praying, as they did five times a day. Islam is the driving force of the Resistance (above)

After the sixth Russian offensive, in August-September 1982, many Panjsher villages were left in ruins, their houses gutted (centre)

Our muj escort at Khenj. He walked from Khenj to Do Ab twice in one night (about 40 miles) without complaint (below)

Russian T72 tank blown up by a mujahideen mine at Bazarak. The force of the explosion tore the gun turret off. The mujahideen boost their Chinese-made mines with additional explosive from unexploded Russian bombs (above)

One of the half-dozen Russian BTR 60 armoured personnel carriers knocked out by mujahideen rocket-propelled grenades (RPG) at Shawa, half-way up the Panjsher Valley, in a bitter engagement in May-June 1982 (below) one side and keeping his voice low, he managed to have a private conversation although surrounded by people. Finally, Masud drew Jean-José to one side. We waited anxiously to hear our fate. He was back in five minutes, his *pattu* over his shoulder like a Roman senator, to announce: 'We are all going now by jeep [cries of delight] to Sangana which is very near. There we will have a hot wash and spend the night. Then tomorrow you, Sandy, Nigel, Charles and Tom and also Tony will go up the valley to Khenj.'

'How far's Khenj?' I asked.

'About thirty kilometres, twenty miles.'

'And what about you and Jean-Philippe?'

'We will stay in Sangana for the moment. He wants to discuss with Jean-Philippe what we will do when and if they have a new hospital and so on.'

I felt slightly irritated that we were to be shunted off to one side, while Jean-José was to remain at the centre of things. However I merely said, 'We rely on you to look after our interests. Can you please make sure Masud does not forget about our equipment?'

'No, no, I have told him already and I will remind him again. He has already given orders to bring it here.'

With that we were dispatched. Masud had already disappeared, so we shouldered our packs and started off down the valley, the river roaring noisily beside us, the rapids ghostly white in the darkness. Luckily we did not have far to walk. Just beside a fair-sized bridge, which to my surprise the Russians had left unblown, our escort turned left, and in the light of his torch we saw the outline of a jeep hidden under a tree. It had two neat bullet holes right through the windscreen which, although starred, was otherwise intact. The mujahideen had apparently captured it during the first offensive earlier in the year by shooting the two occupants dead. We pushed it to start and then clambered in, packed tightly together on the very hard seats. We crossed the bridge and drove down the rocky track to another bridge over the Panjsher River, turned left and with the mountain on our right and the broad river bed on our left, bumped the two or three miles to Sangana, a biggish village just off the road and hidden in a thick clump of trees.

There, we were split up: Tom and Charles going to one house, Tony to another, and Nigel and I to a third. Nigel, although I did not realize it at first, was in the throes of an acute attack of gastro-enteritis and collapsed on the floor as soon as we were shown to our room. It was with great difficulty that I got him up to have his hot wash. This consisted of standing naked on a raised mud floor and pouring warm water over oneself from a large tin. It was the first proper wash we had had since leaving Dean's Hotel and, despite the technical difficulties of the operation, I felt much refreshed at the end of it. We were clearly in a superior household since, in addition to the bath house, there was an open-air lavatory on the flat roof just outside our room. It was merely a hole in the roof over which one squatted, but poor Nigel had to avail himself of it repeatedly during the night.

6

We left Sangana as the sun was coming up, to drive to Khenj. It was a lovely morning, the light softening the harshness of the mountains and making the river sparkle in its broad, stony bed. We passed lots of knocked-out Soviet and Afghan vehicles: three or four T55 tanks, a dozen or more armoured personnel carriers (BTR 60s), and fifteen or so army lorries, some of which had plunged off the road into the river. In places where the road was trapped between the side of the mountain and the steep bank of the Panjsher, the mujahideen had had most success. In one village a whole line of lorries and BTR 60s littered the side of the road and, just outside Shawa, where it makes a hairpin bend over the river, half a dozen personnel carriers had been destroyed and one tank, marooned in the middle of the river, pointed its gun disconsolately at the sky. The mujahideen told us that they had ambushed the Russians from the rocks immediately above, shooting down on them with their RPGs, the portable grenade launchers invented by the Russians and copied so effectively by the Chinese. The mujahideen had stripped the machine guns (DSKs and Zigoyaks) off the BTR 60s and the tanks, and were using them as anti-aircraft guns which they proudly displayed to us. In the village itself, we saw two huge bomb craters beside the road, made by Russian jets the day before, we were told!

Two things impressed me on the drive. One was the stark beauty of the country, softened only by the green splash of the villages. The other was the simple but effective irrigation system, on both sides of the river, which consisted of a water channel running parallel to the river but well above it, from which each village and clump of houses could draw off water for its own fields.

It took us about two hours to reach Khenj, which announced its importance by the row of small shops lining the one and only street. We stopped in the middle of the village and our driver gestured us towards a tea-house. I thought that by now I was fairly hardened to Afghan conditions, but the inside of this particular *chai khana* was almost too much for me on an empty stomach. The walls were almost covered by a dense swarm of flies which, perhaps because of the coolness of the morning (we were now at around nine thousand feet), hardly stirred, managing only short and occasional hops between long periods of immobility. The rest of the tea-house was equally squalid.

While we waited silently for the tea, a figure entered and advanced on us. For a second or two we failed to recognize him, until he thrust a thumbless hand at us to be shaken.

'Jamil', we all cried, with a mixture of surprise and apprehension. For it was the wily and irascible horse-coper whom we had last seen at the crossing of the Kabul River. Tony spoke to him and then explained.

'We're staying in Jamil's house. He wants to take us up to his place now.' Jamil lived in the upper part of the town, well shaded by mulberry and walnut trees. We climbed up a steep flight of stone steps to his house, set against the rock and with a fine view of the lower part of Khenj, the river and the valley beyond. The main living-room bore the scars of Russian rocket fire in the shape of two large holes in the wall, under the eaves. But there were carpets and cushions on the floor and even a bed in the corner on to which Nigel, now looking very sick, wearily sank. Jamil took our dirty clothes off to be washed, and with some pride pointed to the outside privy, sited on the far corner of the flat roof.

Despite the intensity of the Russian summer offensive, the fifth against the Panjsher in three years, we were finding conditions in the valley generally, and the people's morale in particular, much better than we had expected. But prices of food were double or treble what they had been in the Panjsher and elsewhere, and that inevitably meant hardship for the poorer people. In the afternoon we watched Russian jets bombing in the distance at the bottom of the valley, saw them diving steeply and heard the distant explosions.

Next day Jamil took us for a walk through the village. Tom, who seemed to have contracted the same bug as Nigel, stayed behind. We walked down to the river, past a number of houses damaged by bombing, and Jamil gave a long explanation of how the Russians, as well as sending tanks up the valley, had landed airborne troops by helicopter on the tops of two mountains overlooking Khenj. From there they had been able to shoot up the town at will, until, Jamil claimed, after three days the mujahideen managed to get above them and dislodge them. The Russians had held Khenj for three weeks, using it as an advance headquarters and pushing up the valley as far as Dasht-i-Riwat where the road ends.

The part of the town south of the river was very badly bombed, although they were rebuilding one house. Just beyond that a tiny shop was selling quantities of delicious-looking grapes and apples, as well as leather Red Army belts, with the hammer and sickle stamped on the buckle. They must have fallen off a lorry in Kabul, or perhaps had been sold by some crooked quarter-master. In any event, they were cheap at £1. We all bought one. Jamil led us now to a large flat expanse of pebbles by the river where the Russians had parked their tanks, leaving behind the bric-à-brac of occupation: empty Bulgarian ration tins and cartridge cases, as well as some meatier items in the shape of one tank, a waterlogged A.P.C., several lorries and an Afghan mess truck. The mujahideen jumped on top of the wrecked A.P.C. and stood there like big-game hunters on the carcass of an elephant and I found myself joining them. The machine gun had been removed and the inside well and truly gutted. I thought how unpleasant to be inside one that got hit; there seemed to be only one exit and that was very small.

On the way back we came on a group of boys setting fire to Russian ammunition that seemed to be scattered around everywhere. Then they came running past us in file, making a mock attack with home-made models of Russian jets carved from wood. As they passed us they loosed off their 'rockets', cleverly adapted from single bullets, which shot off with a realistic hiss and puff of pink smoke. Jamil and his friends laughed and applauded. I cursed that we did not have the camera and Nigel agreed, enthusing: 'What a marvellous sequence. It tells the whole story. It also tells you something about the Afghans. Those boys have grown up with the war. It's part of their lives. If you could film that, it would make a tremendous impact on a British audience.'

'When we get the camera, we'll come back and shoot it,' I said, although I only half believed my own words. I knew from long experience that, if you did not film something at the time, it almost invariably proved impossible to go back and do it again.

Jamil did his best to feed us well: large quantities of rice appeared at every meal, accompanied by boiled mutton and preceded by rather greasy soup. Nigel, who was still ailing, could only manage some broth and Tom, who spent most of the time sleeping, refused all food. The way in which various members of the family and friends would arrive at meal times to share the food and then linger to talk with our host was very Afghan. But it also meant we had almost no privacy.

By the end of twenty-four hours the rest of us seemed to have succumbed to the prevailing disease and the privy was in almost constant use. Luckily one of the local shops had a good supply of lavatory paper and we were able to replenish our stocks.

I had noticed a barber's shop next to the fly-blown tea-house, so next morning I repaired there for a shave and haircut. I was the only customer. The barber, a small, fierce-looking man, sat me down in front of a cracked mirror and started his preparations: cold water, very little shaving soap and a semi-hairless shaving brush. He rubbed my face very hard to get a lather, without much success, and then produced a cut-throat razor with which he proceeded to scrape my face. The combination of rather blunt razor and too little soap made what can be a luxurious experience a long and rather painful affair. I had failed to get my hair cut before departure and by now it was much too long. The Khenj barber made short work of it, slicing it off in great hunks like an Australian outback sheepshearer. I stood up looking and feeling quite different. When I offered to pay, he waved me away. He was a mujahid, he explained, implying it was an honour to be able to cut my hair. Then it was Tony's turn. His hair was pretty short anyway, but he liked it even shorter and the Khenj maestro was ready to oblige.

Tony was an interesting character. Despite his marked Australian accent, he had been born in England of an English father and French mother, and educated for two years at St Andrews before emigrating to Australia, where he completed his degree. He had also spent a year in China studying Mandarin. Apart from Chinese and French, which he spoke well, he had a good working knowledge of Farsi – which was proving so valuable to us. This was his second trip to Afghanistan and he was knowledgeable about the Resistance. He worked, he said, for *Asia Week*, a news magazine published in Bangkok, where he lived. He was extremely efficient, his rucksack was the model of neatness with everything in its right place, and serious to the point of dourness. We wondered at times if his interest in Afghanistan went beyond pure journalism.

I was sitting in Jamil's room after lunch, gazing out of the window, when I saw two Russian jets diving at great speed. As I followed their progress against the cloudless blue of the Panjsher sky, they pulled out of the dive and started climbing. I was idly wondering what they were playing at when there were two powerful explosions and we rushed outside to the terrace to see brown smoke and dust rising high in the air. The jets had dropped their bombs on the near side of Kharru, a village perched on the side of the hill about two miles away, its fields making a pretty splash of green against the mountain. Above the village, a torrent toppled over the top of the cliff in a glittering cascade. Through the binoculars we could see the bombs had hit a group of houses on the edge of a steep gully. Damage seemed to be considerable. Jamil became very excited, especially when two more clusters of bombs went off, one of them behind Kharru, sending up a lot of smoke.

At four o'clock, a clutch of helicopters and jets (MIG 23s or SU 25s) returned to the attack, this time strafing another village further down the valley. I guessed it might be Shawa, where the mujahideen had so proudly displayed their captured machine guns to us on our way up. We could see the jets making repeated runs and the smoke rising above the 'V' of the valley. It was difficult to know which were more dangerous, the jets or the helicopters. The jets were probably more frightening, as they dived with a terrifying howl of their engines. But the helicopters looked more deadly. After dropping their bombs, they circled and came in to rocket the target and spray it with their multiple cannon, which made a deep bloodthirsty sound like a giant burping.

By the end of the afternoon Jamil, who was volatile at the best of times, was extremely jumpy and told Tony the Russians must know he had foreigners in his house! He was convinced the Russians would bomb Khenj next, so he warned us to be ready to leave the house at six next morning. This we did, munching a dry piece of bread but without the comfort of a cup of tea. We crossed the river by the wooden bridge and climbed out of the village up a side valley, passing a low stone building covered in fine white dust – the local flour mill. Lots of women and children and quite a few men were taking the same route, making for caves and shelters higher up.

At seven the jets made their first appearance of the day, bombing a village further up the main valley. An hour later they made another strike, and from our vantage point on the side of the hill we could see the smoke climbing above the mountain tops. Each time the jets appeared the Afghans became very panicky, which was understandable as they travelled at such speed and with such a demoralizing scream that they were on to us before we knew it. The attack nearly always came as a surprise. We heard that six people had been killed and nine wounded at a village called Zinneh the previous day.

Moving higher up the side valley in pursuit of food, we installed ourselves in a shady spot beside the river and breakfasted off the mulberry trees. There was a solitary house on the hillside above, which appeared to belong to a very friendly old man and his son. After the old man had inspected us to his satisfaction, the son reappeared bearing a tray with a thermos full of freshly brewed tea and *nan*. A cloth was spread on the stones and we had brunch, watched with great curiosity by some old men with long beards, leathery faces and shrewd eyes. One had a badly swollen foot and made the usual mistake of thinking we were doctors. But, despite their unfailing hospitality, there was no doubt that the Afghan peasants regarded us to some extent as Jonahs who were more likely than not to attract Russian fire. Jamil, for example, was convinced that Government spies in Khenj had already reported our presence and that retribution would follow.

Whether he was right or not, at about eleven there was another strike, with the jets rocketing the main valley below us, and then at about half-past two they came back and started bombing Khenj. I counted three jets which made six or eight passes, dropping eighteen to twenty bombs in the space of about fifteen minutes. They came in high from the west, diving steeply with a terrifying howl, and released their bombs just before they reached the bottom of the dive. The air was so pristine that, despite the distance, we could see the sinister black bomblets leave the belly of the plane and follow their descent to the target below. The first bombs fell on the upper part of the town (we could imagine the state that Jamil would be in now!) and then they turned their attention to the area beside the river. The explosions reverberated up the valley – we could actually feel the shock waves – and the smoke rose like a desert storm. We knew that the mujahideen had a 'Dashaka' machine gun dug into the rocky spur just above the main valley and we could hear it firing in short bursts amid the roar of the jets.

Having a grandstand view of the attack made it doubly infuriating that we were not able to film it. Late in the afternoon, seething with frustration, we set off back to Khenj, where the smoke was still rising into the untroubled blue sky. I was determined somehow to reach Masud and insist on getting our cameras. Tony said he would come with me. As we neared the bottom of the side valley, we passed an enormous bomb crater. The blast had mutilated the trees and hurled great splinters of rock about like shrapnel. Just opposite was the hill where the Dashaka had been sited and, in their attempts to wipe out the machine-gun post, the Russians had flattened the whole area.

We were just climbing over a wall when we heard the angry voice of our escort. Almost gibbering with rage and concern, he kept pointing to the crater and to the sky. Tony said finally: 'He's very, very upset. He says it is too dangerous to go back into Khenj. It's his duty to protect us and he is ordering us not to go on, I think.' Tony added on his own account: 'We have a crisis on our hands. We'll have to go along with him.'

I was reluctant to give in: 'Well, what does he want us to do?'

'He wants to go to a house which is just up the hill behind us. We can spend the night there, he says, and then decide what to do next.'

There was not really an alternative, so we climbed up a steep path (as Nigel said, it was always up in Afghanistan) to a house directly opposite the Dashaka position. There were bullet holes in the walls, although whether from that day or a previous encounter was not clear. The owner was a *mast* (yoghurt) specialist and fed us two or three different kinds – all delectable. Tom and Nigel asked our escort, now restored to his normal smiling self, if they could walk down to the town to buy cigarettes and, to my surprise, he agreed. I would like to have gone too, but thought it wiser to stay behind as a kind of hostage.

When they came back an hour later, they said the bombing had caused a lot of damage. The flour mill had been hit and flour was scattered all over the place. They had seen Jamil, who said his house had been hit and was now convinced beyond all doubt that spies had reported our presence and that the air raid was a direct consequence. Whatever credit our presence might once have conferred was now clearly exhausted. All this reinforced my determination to try to reach Masud; so after supper, around nine, Tony and I set off with a slightly reluctant escort to walk down the valley.

We were soon through Khenj and striding down the road at a good pace with a moon to light our way. The country was serenely beautiful, the sharp outline of the mountains a mere blur, the sound of the river a constant accompaniment on our left. I had recovered from the rigours of the inward march and I felt fit and strong and ready to walk all night if necessary. We passed Zinneh, Shawa, Omarz, with only a brief stop at a mujahideen command post and were well down the road to Do Ab, where the Darra joins the Panjsher, when we suddenly saw a faint beam of light among the trees. It turned out to be a mujahideen lorry going up the valley. We slogged on down the road. The moon set around eleven and we had been going for about an hour in the dark, when more lights appeared in the distance. They came towards us rapidly, tilting up and down as the vehicle bounced over the potholes. As it drew abreast we saw it was Masud's Russian jeep with the bullet holes through the windscreen and his driver at the wheel. Sitting beside him, his piratical profile immediately recognizable, was Agha Gul. We were bidden to get in behind, leaving a very angry escort to walk back to Khenj, and set off at a fast pace, bumping and lurching through the night. Agha Gul explained to Tony that they had been coming to fetch us from Khenj on Masud's orders.

'Why?'

'Because the Russians have started their attack.'

I felt a sharp stab of apprehension. Masud's information had been absolutely right. He had said within a week: it was, in fact, four days later.

We crossed the big bridge at Do Ab and drove towards the smaller bridge on the Darra, where we had started our journey a few nights before. There we got out and followed Agha Gul down a path to a house standing by itself. Dogs barked noisily as we were led across the courtyard and up the stairs. At the top, one of the very few fat Afghans we encountered was waiting with a lamp in his hand. He unlocked a door and, holding his lamp high, showed us in. The room was full of recumbent bodies which stirred uneasily at this untimely interruption. I recognized the big sergeant-major, who made space for us to lie down and then, as my eyes grew accustomed to the dimness, I saw that Masud was stretched out beside the wall at the

far end of the room, apparently quite oblivious to our arrival. I lay
down on the carpet, pulled the *pattu* which someone proffered around
me and almost instantly was fast asleep.

Only a few minutes later, or so it seemed, we were woken by
movement in the room. In the lamplight I saw that Masud was
pulling on his boots and that the rest of his entourage were ready to
depart. (Afghans dress more quickly in the morning than anyone I
have ever seen: of course they do not dress, in Western terms, they
merely adjust their dress.) Masud was clearly in a hurry and I was
not sure that he had seen us so, as he made for the door, I stepped
forward.

'*Bonjour*,' I said. He stopped and took my hand.

'Ah, bonjour. Ça va?'

'Are we going with you?'

'We are all going together. The Russian offensive started
yesterday. They have a lot of tanks and men further down the valley
at Bazarak.' Bazarak was the next town to Rokha, the Russians'
jumping-off point. A second later Masud was out of the door and
clattering down the stairs.

We followed, crossing the bridge in the dark and then heading up
river again towards the brothers' house. This time we did not stop,
but walked fast for half an hour or so until we reached the centre of
Tambonnah. A light was on in a big house in the middle of the village
square and a line of people was queuing up to go inside – whether for
weapons or medicines, I could not make out. But there was a general
air of urgency, and after a short rest the big sergeant-major told us to
follow him. Masud had disappeared. After about two hours' steady
climbing we came to a small group of houses clinging to the steep side
of the mountain like swallows' nests. We circled round the houses
and clambered up a steep rocky slope to a cave, the entrance so well
hidden that it was almost undetectable from a distance. Inside, it
opened out to accommodate four or five people. A local farmer
spread a rug on the floor and brought a couple of overstuffed pillows
and we made ourselves as comfortable as possible.

Masud suddenly appeared at nine and crawled into the cave. He
was much less alarmed by the Russian attack than I would have
expected: in fact, I found his calm reassuring and impressive. He
said the Russians had sent three hundred tanks, A.P.C.s and lorries
up the valley from Rokha towards Bazarak and that four had already
been destroyed by mujahideen mines. He believed they planned to

attack as far as Khenj (poor Jamil). Masud gave a figure of between sixty and seventy civilians killed in the air raids. I asked him about aid from the West and he said categorically: 'We are getting no help at all from the West.'

He departed as suddenly as he had come, leaving behind his elder brother Yahya, who spoke good English, to look after us. Yahya studied to be a vet for three years at Kabul University before the Communist takeover of 1978. He had been in jail for eight months as a political prisoner of the Communists before managing to escape to the Panjsher. I asked him how he had learnt his English.

'I got a British Council scholarship for a year.'

I felt enormously grateful to that much-criticized body at that moment. Not only would Yahya be extremely useful as an interpreter but what better way to ensure access to the leader himself?

Just after two, we were rudely disturbed by the crescendo howl of a jet engine and the incredibly vicious crack of rockets being fired very close. Yahya, who was sitting nearest the mouth of the cave, threw himself to one side and even I, sitting right at the back, the living rock covering me like a tomb, felt a twinge of terror.

The suddenness and noise of the attack were quite terrifying. The unseen jet made three more runs, each time unleashing a brace of rockets with ear-splitting effect. Could the Russians know that Masud was here? After all, why attack this remote spot rather than a hundred other places in the Panjsher Valley? I began to wonder if their intelligence was better than we thought.

When the attacks were over, we scrambled out of the cave to find a house at the bottom of the valley still burning. There was no sign of Masud but we gathered he was in another cave. We spent the rest of the afternoon admiring the magnificent view and talking to Yahya. In an effort to impress him, and by extension Masud, I talked about the important effect our documentary could have on public and Government opinion in Britain, and elsewhere. Yahya listened attentively and said they were very keen (meaning Masud and his Panjsheri Resistance Movement) to have direct contact with Western governments.

As the sun declined, the colours changed entrancingly; the stark browns and shale greys of the mountains softening to umber and purple, the green of the river line glowing like a linnet's wing, the blue of the sky deepening with that peculiar intensity only possible at altitude. It would have been idyllic if it had not been for the war: it did not bother us again that afternoon, but we saw the jets performing their lethal aerobatics in the distance while we waited for Nigel, Charles and Tom to arrive.

In the evening we walked down the hill and up the other side to a small village. After supper we were shown our sleeping quarters, a flat roof open to the stars. We had to cross a narrow plank to get to it, which was easy in the daytime but trickier at night. Masud left at around midnight – Yahya said that he always worked at night when there was fighting. As we got ready to sleep there was still no sign of the others, and it was not until three that I woke to find the exhausted trio stumbling about, trying to find a space to lie down. It had taken them nine hours, with stops, to walk from Khenj. The mujahid escort had walked all the way back after leaving us with Agha Gul and, after a brief rest, had started off down the valley again with them. He seemed unmoved by his exertions.

We were woken at about five by the sound of Russian mortars or rockets exploding further down the valley and Yahya urged us to hurry; although we did have time for tea and *nan*. It was before seven when we saw the first Russian air activity of the day; four helicopters circling over the main valley. They flew high and slowly, but with the ominous precision of a hornet, choosing their target with infinite care and with the sure knowledge that nothing could attack them. These MI-24s are heavily armoured underneath; the only vulnerable area is the plexiglass cockpit, so unless a mujahid machine gunner can get above the helicopter, he has very little chance of shooting one down.

We climbed back up the hill to our cave, but found that it was now occupied by some women and children. Yahya cast around for the cave where Masud had hidden, but failed to find it and we spent the rest of the day rather uncomfortably, in the shelter of a huge rock. While the exhausted travellers slept, I had a long conversation with Yahya about his family.

His father had been a colonel in the Afghan Army and, depending on his postings, the family had lived all over the country. Their mother had been a strong character, exerting a lot of influence on her children, and had taught herself to read and write when she was middle-aged. Masud had gone to primary school in Herat, near the Iranian border, and then to the Istiqlal Lycée, run by the French, in Kabul. He had wanted to enter the Military Academy but went instead to the Polytechnic in Kabul where he studied engineering for

three years. Then in 1973, when Masud was nineteen, Daoud, a
cousin of the King and former Prime Minister, seized power,
banished the monarchy and set Afghanistan on a course that was to
bring it much closer to the Soviet Union. In 1975, a group of anti-
Communist insurgents (including Masud, then twenty-one) staged
a coup against Daoud, which succeeded in the Panjsher Valley but
failed nationally. Masud fled to Pakistan where he spent the next
three years studying guerrilla warfare and, according to Yahya,
received training from friends in the Pakistan Army.

Early in 1979, with opposition to the new Communist régime
becoming nationwide, Masud slipped back into Kabul and went
underground. He was there when the Russians invaded in December
and immediately set off back to the Panjsher to organize the
Resistance. He started with only a handful of men but by dint of
sheer determination and personality had, in the short space of three
years and despite constant Russian attacks (this was the sixth), built
up a coherent guerrilla army of fifteen hundred men, double what it
was in 1981. The Russians launched their first offensive against the
Panjsher in 1980, three more in 1981, and the fifth, a very heavy
attack, in May 1982.

Sitting in the shade of a huge rock, with the sun scorching the bare
hillside around us, Yahya let drop a significant remark. I knew that
the fragmentary nature of the Resistance was one of its greatest
weaknesses, so I asked him if Masud had any ambitions to become a
national leader.

'He doesn't want to,' Yahya said, fixing me with his one good,
dark brown eye (the other strayed). 'But he realizes that one day he
must try and build a national movement based on his Panjsher
organization. You know that leaders come from all over Afghanistan
to ask Masud to give them a commander to lead their men. He
instructs them also how they should fight the Russians. He tells them
to attack the big bases. We have already made two attacks on
Bagram and one in Jebel Sarraj [near the Panjsher]. In the two
attacks on Bagram we destroyed thirty-nine helicopters and jets on
the ground.'

I took Yahya's figures with a pinch of salt, but the suggestion that
Masud might be a second Tito did not sound so far-fetched after all.

7

A bad night on the flat roof: an artillery shell went off at around midnight, jolting me out of a delightful slumber. It sounded uncomfortably close, but it would have to have been extremely close to get me up in the middle of the night. More followed at roughly half-hourly intervals and then at five we all got up and made ready for a quick departure, delaying only to perform the daily miracle of popping our genies back in their bottles. Just before we walked the plank back to *terra firma* for the last time, a salvo of rockets landed on the hillside below us, sending up innocent-looking puffs of smoke. Yahya, who was anxious already, became extremely nervous and urged us to hurry.

At 5.30, toiling upwards, we saw several helicopters overflying the valley below. As we climbed, one thought bubbled in my mind, coming and going with my laboured breathing: we were moving away from the Russians but also further away from wherever our equipment was. What was happening about the equipment anyway? *Pant.* No one knew. *Pant. Pant.* Yahya could offer no real information; Masud had disappeared on more urgent matters and we were being driven along, like spume before the wind, by the Russian advance.

The latest reports said that the Russians had pushed through Bazarak and were now in Astana, the next small town where the French hospital, a big stone house, used to be. Two other French hospital buildings had been bombed by the Russians, so the French had asked the International Red Cross if they could paint a red cross on the roof. Approval was granted, the cross was duly painted and almost immediately the Russians bombed it. The building had been evacuated during the summer offensive but last year, Jean-José explained nostalgically, it had been a real haven. A former chef at the French Embassy in Kabul, a certain Mr Siddiqi, had cooked *steack avec frites* for the residents, who included any journalists who happened to be visiting the Panjsher. Alas, in three weeks we had eaten little but rice, *nan* and goat, and would have been delighted to have made Mr Siddiqi's acquaintance.

After an hour of hard walking we reached a village high up the side valley. We were taken to a small farmhouse overlooking a paddock, shaded by enormous mulberry and walnut trees, above a river. Huge rocks, which must have come crashing down the valley in a more tempestuous age, were scattered about everywhere. A villager just back from Kabul gave us, through Yahya, a fascinating account of the situation in the capital. He said the mujahideen had made one suburb a no-go area, there had been fighting in another and they had retaken Paghman, a town outside Kabul. The Russians and their Afghan allies were obliged to stick to the main roads, even in Kabul. Press gangs were active, rounding up all men between thirty-six and forty-two for the Army. He also claimed that there was a split in the Government over the latest attack on the Panjsher, with Babrak Karmal's wing of the Communist Party, known as Parcham (meaning Flag), for it and the rival Khalq (Masses) against it: the Khalqis arguing that the previous offensive had killed only women and children and that another attack would alienate the civilian population even more.

'There has been a big movement towards the mujahideen,' he said. 'Only old men and children are left in Kabul now.' According to the talk in the bazaars, there had been a shoot-out at a recent party meeting: three ministers had been killed and several others wounded, including Babrak Karmal. A week after the alleged shooting, Babrak Karmal had appeared on Afghan television looking distinctly shaky, our informant added gleefully. Of course it was impossible to know how much to believe. Our journalistic caution tended to make us sceptical of most figures and claims, and undoubtedly Afghans have a cavalier way with numbers.

On the other hand, there was nothing wildly improbable about suggestions of a gun fight at party headquarters. Babrak Karmal's predecessor, Hafizullah Amin, who had murdered scores of people and been gunned down himself by the Russians when they invaded. Afghan politics had long had a reputation for being bloodthirsty.

Even the Russians had not escaped entirely. The Russian general who supervised the invasion in December 1979 was said to have shot himself shortly afterwards.

But in the midst of this euphoria, Yahya sounded a cautioning note. There was danger of starvation in the Panjsher in the coming winter, he told me.

'The Russians are applying a scorched earth policy. They are burning the crops, the houses, everything. We appeal to the United Nations and to Western governments to help us.' (His forecast was to turn out to be distressingly accurate.)

After we had breakfasted, we were chivvied out of the house by the diminutive householder and led up the mountain. The bleak hillside stretched upwards remorselessly in front of us and I felt a sudden surge of rebellion. I was also beginning to feel unpleasantly weak.

'Where exactly are we going?' I demanded angrily.

'To a cave,' Yahya said with infuriating calm.

'Yes, but where, exactly?' I had to struggle to control my breathing as we laboured up the slope. It was Yahya's turn to become tetchy.

'Here, just in front, it's not far.' He pointed to a massive rock, the size of a house, about a quarter of a mile away. Under its overhang I could make out the dark mouth of a cave. A sort of helpless gloom settled over us at the thought of another day in a cave, another day without our camera gear, indeed another day in which we would be making no visible progress towards recovering it.

It was in a thoroughly frustrated frame of mind that I struggled up the last incline to the cave. Inside it was roomy but extremely cold, so I decided to sit outside. At least I would improve my tan while I read one of our paperbacks. This, however, was too dull for Tony and Charles and they decided to climb to the top of the ridge above us to get a view of the main valley and possibly of the Russian advance. They were gone for several hours but, when they eventually returned, they were full of excitement at what they had seen: eighty to a hundred Russian and Afghan vehicles (tanks, A.P.C.s and lorries) crossing the river near Do Ab. Jets were strafing the hills on both sides of the road, and mortars and artillery were shelling the entrance to the Darra Valley. They had taken some pictures with their still cameras, but Charles said they were so far away that they would only be tiny dots. On the way down, a helicopter gunship had flown dangerously close. They were not sure if it had spotted them, but they had decided to run for it and had escaped. We heard later that jets had bombed the Darra Valley, including Abdullah Kheil, presumably in preparation for a ground attack.

We returned to our host's house at dusk and were sitting rather disconsolately, with our backs to the wall (very apposite), waiting for the women, who had also been hiding in caves all day, to make supper, when there was a commotion outside. A man burst into the room with a shiny metal box on his back.

'It's the spare boards,' Tom and Charles said with one accord. These were the spare electronic brains of the camera, valued at around £12,000. We all rose to our feet and hurled questions at the stranger. But Yahya was unable to elicit much and he could tell us nothing about the rest of the equipment.

'He was given this box and told to carry it down to us. He comes from near Abdullah Kheil.'

However, I reasoned, the message was clear. If one piece had been found, the rest could not be far away.

'Let's get up early and walk to Abdullah Kheil,' I said. Tom volunteered to come with me.

Yahya, who had at first said it was too dangerous because of the Russian bombing, finally, but reluctantly gave way to our insistence. Tony was also het up, being caught as usual in the middle, having to translate one side's argument to the other.

'Yahya is not happy, not happy at all about you going up the Darra on your own. He insists that you don't all walk in a bunch, but spaced out, fifty yards apart.'

'Okay,' I said. 'I'll start, then Tom, and Charles and Nigel can come on behind.' Tony and Jean-José, who had rejoined us, were to stay behind with Yahya.

We left at six and within half an hour there was a lot of Russian activity, especially from the four-engined Antonov reconnaissance plane, which made a particularly sinister drone and which, the Afghans were convinced, could spot a man on the ground from half a mile up.

On our way down we came on a group of mujahideen taking cover from the Antonov. Unusually for them, their handshakes were limp and their expressions dejected. We heard later that they had put up a poor performance the previous night, allowing Russian airborne troops to outflank them and had received a tongue-lashing from Masud. Indeed, he had climbed in the dark to the scene of the action

and personally taken command. I had not seen him in this light
before: he had struck me more as a thinking general who stayed in
the background.

'He was very angry,' Yahya told us later. 'He went up with just a
few men and took over the battle.'

Apart from the Antonov, we saw a lot of helicopters flying up the
main valley, first a dozen, then ten, then five, possibly ferrying
reinforcements or supplies to the airborne troops, who were said to
have been flown to Khenj the day before.

The shiny aluminium of the spare boards' case would have made a
good heliograph, so we wrapped it in a *pattu* and lugged it in turn.
Although not particularly heavy, it was awkward to carry; but
despite it we made good time.

Once again I was ravished by the beauty of the Darra, the fields
ripening in the sun under a cloudless blue sky. At the bridge over the
limpid pool we turned left up a side valley, climbing through patches
planted with potatoes and root crops. The maize field at the top was
bright with poppies, but there was something ominous about the
utter tranquillity. Then I realized that there was absolutely no one
about. The village opposite was empty. It was as if a Russian attack
were imminent and everyone had fled up the mountain. We
clambered round a huge new crater at the corner of the maize field.
The blast had flattened some of the stalks and we scooped up a few of
the fallen heads. A hundred yards further on we came to the *qarârgâh*
in a secondary school. It was also empty, silent and undamaged
apart from a few rocket holes on one outside wall. It seemed such an
obvious target that we decided to make temporary camp a few
hundred yards away below the maize field. There, in a meadow full
of tall blue-flowered clover, we lay down to wait for the others. It was
an idyllic scene, the scent of the clover almost overpowering, the
river singing in the sunshine below us.

Nigel and Charles arrived half an hour later. We were all so
hungry we decided we would have a proper meal for once. A stream
ran through the *qarârgâh* and we could make a fire there. Nigel, as
soupmaster, borrowed one of the mujahideen's pots and started
heating two of Mr Knorr's packets – one of ham and pea, the other of
asparagus. Charles was in charge of potatoes, which I had pulled out
of the field, and maize. Nigel found some tea in the storeroom but his
culinary expertise did not extend that far. Before I could stop him he
had tipped three or four large spoonfuls into the boiling kettle.

'Hey, hold on,' I cried. 'That's far too much.'

'Why is it too much?' he asked.

'Well,' I said, 'normally you reckon only one or at most two teaspoonfuls for a teapot. You must know that from making it at home.'

'I've never made a cup of tea in my life before,' Nigel said calmly, 'so I've absolutely no idea how many spoonfuls you need.'

The first cupful was just tolerable but after that the strength of the brew defied even our great thirst. Still, the rest of the meal was the best we had had for days and we lay back on a rickety *charpoy*, not even minding the flies that settled on us with lazy persistence.

At one point an Afghan came in, gave us an accusing glance and left again after locking the tea cupboard. We washed out the pot as thoroughly as possible (ham is anathema to Muslims) and, before leaving, inspected every room for signs of our equipment. One room on the ground floor was locked, but I was able to peer through the cracks in the door: nothing of ours was inside.

We returned to our clover field and reclined in the shade, admiring the landscape. All around us, I noted, the Panjsheris had terraced their stony fields with enormous industry: Afghanistan must be the stoniest country in the world, an Asian version of the Highlands. On the opposite side of the river, fields of brilliant yellow mustard and dark green clover glowed like a Van Gogh painting in the afternoon sun. Now and again a solitary mujahid would hurry along the track to the village, asleep on its rock above the river; but there was no other sign of life.

Charles was the first to walk down to the river to wash and came back saying it was wonderfully refreshing. The big green pool that looked so inviting was a bomb crater, he reported, and a recent one at that. Spurred by his example, the rest of us followed and, taking off all our clothes except for our underpants (you never knew, a mullah might just be watching) plunged into the pool. The water was so cold it made me gasp. It was our first real wash for a week or ten days and we emerged feeling marvellously clean and alive.

Alas, we now became involved in a long and tedious argument about whether to stay where we were and wait for Yahya, who might or might not be on his way up, or continue up the valley to Abdullah Kheil, where, if my hunch was right, the rest of our equipment was to be found. The argument was finally ended by a decision to split up. Charles and I would walk on up the valley, while Nigel and Tom would stay so as to rendezvous with Yahya and the others, if that proved possible, and come on the following day.

Charles and I set off at around 3.30 and soon fell in with a young muj. After two hours' steady walking uphill he led us across the river to the house of the commander of the Abdullah Kheil mujahideen. At the foot of the very steep slope that led to his house our muj stopped to talk to a young man who was eating apricots. When he saw we were hungry (again) he shook the tree above us and rained down dozens of apricots, rather small and dry, but very acceptable.

The Commander, or *malik* as they called him, was a senior, courteous figure who lived in a big fortress-like house at the top of the hill. We were taken in through the kitchen, where the veiled women of the house were hard at work over an open fire, and ushered into a big room overlooking the valley. Various friends and neighbours rose to their feet to welcome us, including the local mullah. We produced our piece of paper from Yahya, which requested help in the search for our equipment, and they all sat deciphering and discussing it by the light of the solitary lamp. But it was only after supper that a younger man who spoke some German said: 'There's a mujahid here who says your cameras are at Tunkhu.'

'Tunkhu, where's that?' I asked.

'Here,' he replied pointing across the valley, 'not far.' I could hardly control my excitement.

'How does he know that our equipment is there?' I asked.

There followed a quick passage in Farsi and then: 'He was at Tunkhu himself and saw it. Some black boxes, he says.'

Charles and I were by now thoroughly excited but unable to elicit any more information. 'The Commander says he will send a mujahid with you tomorrow to find your equipment.'

At around 9.30 they all got up, shook hands and left to fight the Russians in the direction of Bazarak. I reckoned this would have meant climbing right up the mountain to twelve thousand feet and then down the other side. They left in high spirits, as if they had been going to a party.

At around midnight Charles and I were woken by a burst of mortars or rockets on the hillside opposite. They must have been fired from the main valley over the intervening mountain wall, but aimed at random; what the Americans in Vietnam used to call H 'n I (Harassment and Interdiction).

At 5.45 we had a repeat performance from mortars or howitzers and this time saw the smoke rising on the hillside opposite. Although no damage seemed to have been done, the explosions lent a certain urgency to our movements. Too much in my case. We had discovered that, in keeping with his elevated station in life, the Commander boasted an outside privy and I repaired there after breakfast. It was sited in rustic simplicity under a huge mulberry tree, beside an irrigation channel, and was solidly constructed of stone and timber. The doorway was, however, extremely low and in my rush to leave I failed to bend down far enough and struck the top of my head such a blow that I was thrown backwards, right on to the business area, so to speak. I lay for a moment half stunned, trying to assess the damage; then got up groggily, rubbing the top of my head, and inspected my long shirt and baggy trousers. Luckily they seemed only a little dusty. So, bending very low this time, I made my exit.

Our escort turned out to be the apricot-shaker of the night before. It was a beautiful morning, with the valley bathed in gentle early sunshine, which gave the whole scene a look of extraordinary innocence. On our way down to the river, our guide stopped and shouted up at a solitary farmhouse. A young man appeared. More shouted conversation and he reappeared with a blue and white bag under his arm. As he came down the slope towards us, Charles became very excited.

'Hey, that's my bag. My personal bag.'

I was equally thrilled, although we were both disappointed that there was only the one. Our guide seemed to know what he was doing, so we followed him across the river and up the other side.

We had just sat down to rest under a tree at the edge of a field when we heard an explosion further down the valley. A Russian jet, a black streak against the clear blue sky, was climbing steeply after releasing its bombs. Smoke rose in the still air. We heard another explosion and the second plane was climbing high up into the sky, trailing its jet stream like a wake behind it. Charles and I sat under our tree thinking the same thing: they were bombing the *qarârgâh*, where we had left Tom and Nigel. The jets circled and dived again. Booom. Booom. A few minutes later they struck again, but further down the valley. The smoke now covered the end of it like light cloud.

Charles was rummaging in his bag like a schoolboy when I happened to glance down the valley and saw two jets coming straight for us, very fast and absolutely silently.

'Get down,' I shouted and they were on us with a terrifying howl. I was standing at the edge of the field below a huge rock and on the wrong side for cover. I threw myself forward, aiming for a small hollow at the foot of the rock, and as I squeezed in I heard a tremendous bang, and saw dust and rock rising from the river bed below me, where there were two or three houses. As I looked back from my upside down position I saw rocks, as big as outsize cannon balls, executing lazy parabolas in the sky, and wondered in a panicky way if they would fall on top of me. I watched one large boulder particularly anxiously and was relieved to see it land in the field with a great thump, seventy-five yards away. Smaller missiles fell closer. I stood up nervously and clambered up to join the others. Charles had half his personal kit strewn on the ground under the trees and was crowing with delight at the emergence of each fresh treasure. He found some Kendal Mint Cake and passed it round the small party of locals who had gathered, drawn by some sixth sense, to inspect the strangers.

At eight, the jets made another attack on the *qarârgâh* and again we wondered anxiously about Nigel and Tom. Charles was busy throwing away the now useless Autoload film, when I saw a man come hurrying down the hill, carrying on his shoulder the cheap, brown leather suitcase we had bought in Pakistan to house the smallest of our three recorders, the BVU 50. We both stood up in excitement and cheered him home as if he had been a victorious marathon runner. Charles quickly undid the case and pronounced the recorder in working order.

Despite the language problem, we gathered he had portered it in from Boularenn and taken it to his own house for safe keeping. A nasty thought was already blighting my delight: if all the porters had done the same thing, our equipment must be scattered far and wide, across the valley. Charles now sat down and drew a list of all our gear, which elicited cries of recognition from some of the onlookers. One worthy, with a splendid old British Lee Enfield from the 1860s, seemed to be saying that he had two of our black boxes, and I was just trying to urge him to go and get them when there came the terrifying howl of a dive-bombing jet and we threw ourselves down. Two bombs exploded 250 yards beyond us, beside another group of houses. Charles had his Pentax in his personal bag and he was feverishly trying to load it when the next jet was on us; there was another terrific explosion and the shrapnel swished through the leaves above us, slicing off small branches. They attacked as a pair,

then climbed away up over the mountains, turned and came racing
up the valley again. Booom. The smoke and the dust rose like a pall
in front of us. After the third or fourth pass, I shouted at Charles:
'Keep down. Don't take too many risks for stills.' Then the man with
the Lee Enfield and I ran across the field to a gully, which gave some
cover. The jets came racing in every two or three minutes to drop
their brace of bombs, the blast bouncing off the rocks above us. Some
were of the airburst variety – designed to explode above the ground
scattering lethal shrapnel – and they made a terrific bang. Charles
had bravely stayed behind beneath his tree, photographing away
like mad. Thank God he did. His stills of the bombing, with Nigel's,
were to make, perhaps, the key sequence of the film.

When the strike was over I emerged cautiously from the gully, just
in time to see two undoubtedly European figures walking
unconcernedly up the path. For a moment I was not sure and then I
shouted, 'Tom, Nigel, thank God you're safe.' In fact they had had a
narrow escape that morning. They had breakfasted in the *qarârgâh*
and had just left when the Russians attacked, scoring several direct
hits and almost destroying the building. They also bombed the
bridge just after Nigel and Tom had crossed it. One bomb had been
very close. Nigel was full of praise for an old woman who had brought
them some hot *nan* at the edge of a field, while the jets were diving on
them like Stukas.

'It was amazing,' he said. 'I think she was so terrified that giving
us something to eat took her mind off what was happening.'

We sat down under the trees to take stock. We had now recovered
five bags including the recorder, video tapes and batteries, but no
camera. I had a feeling that maybe it was in the top village, called
Khoja, where we had spent our first night in the Panjsher. Nigel and
I decided to walk there in the afternoon.

The valley lay silent in the hot sun, held in a sort of midsummer
hush. The morning's bombing had driven most people up into the
mountains and we passed a number of deserted farms. A frightened
cat darted past us looking for the way into one house and became
agitated when it found the door barred. The Antonov, that dire
precursor of every air strike, droned above us. We passed two
Afghans who looked at us with amazement and pointed to the sky.

'Bam, Russ bam,' they chorused, and indicated we should take
cover. We brushed them aside and strode on. But not very far.
Without warning a bomb exploded right beside us and

simultaneously a jet screamed overhead. We threw ourselves down beside the path. Seconds later the second jet screamed down on us. I heard one bomb go off and I was just getting to my feet when a second exploded with ear-splitting force. I cursed my foolishness and was telling myself: 'That's how you get hit' when two black objects – crows or shrapnel? – flashed across my vision from right to left. These were the closest yet, a mere fifty or a hundred yards away. We both realized we were rather exposed.

'Come on, let's find some cover,' I panted to Nigel. We crossed the path and scrambled up into a wheatfield, with a big stone terrace wall surmounted by a tree, on our left. The jets were attacking left to right, down valley, with the sun behind them, so it should give us some protection. The two Afghans who had tried to warn us were now clambering up the hillside in front, shouting encouragement to one another. We had only gone twenty or thirty yards when there was another terrifying jet scream and we threw ourselves down on the soft earth at the foot of the wall.

After an inordinately long pause there came an ear-splitting explosion – the airburst again. I could imagine the jagged shards of metal scything their way across the fields with deadly effect. Nigel and I had both pressed our faces into the ground. As we sat up Nigel said: 'I can't say I terribly enjoyed my mud pack facial.'

We heard a plaintive bleat and a goat stepped delicately towards us, plainly as alarmed as we were.

'Hallo goat, are you frightened?' Nigel enquired, but further conversation was stopped by the vicious scream of a diving SU 25 and two more loud explosions. The goat bleated pathetically and jumped over us – heading in the direction of the bombing. I flattened myself in terror, pressing my face into the friendly grass.

Eventually silence came back, dropping slowly into the valley: we stood up, brushed the mud off our clothes and said farewell to the poor goat which was still looking quite lost. From the path we could see two huge craters in the field just below us; at least fifty yards from a group of houses which were presumably the target. Only one house seemed to have been hit, but not destroyed.

As we continued our interrupted walk, I reflected that the Russians were not very good shots and wondered if they were trainee pilots cutting their bombing teeth on Afghan villages. There were certainly no military targets in the Darra Valley, except for the *qarârgâh*. I was, once more, reminded forcibly of Vietnam. There, whole areas deemed to be under Vietcong control were designated 'free fire zones', which meant that American jets and helicopters could shoot them up at will. Anyone in the free fire zone, man, woman or child, was automatically considered a legitimate target. Quite clearly, the Russians considered the whole of the Panjsher Valley just such a zone. We just happened to be in the middle of it on a particularly busy day.

As we passed another farmhouse, a man appeared, greeted us effusively and pointed proudly to a tree house where, strange though it seemed, he had apparently taken refuge during the bombing. He then invited us to drink tea but, driven by the quest for the camera, I declined and almost immediately regretted it. An invitation to tea usually meant food as well and we had hardly eaten all day.

We trudged on in the afternoon heat, reaching Khoja, the top village, at around three. It appeared to be absolutely deserted, the houses locked and the fields empty. We sat down exhausted, very hungry and thirsty. Nigel then discovered a small group of men on the far side of the village and came back in high hopes of another tea invitation. It turned out though, that they were more interested in showing us the damage to their property. Some very big bombs had been dropped on the upper part of the village, one smashing down a huge old tree and another making a crater twenty feet deep in the middle of a field. The blast had smashed the door and the windows of the nearest house, scattering earth and debris inside as if it had been hit by a hurricane.

Later we were offered tea by a powerful black-browed farmer with magazine pictures of the former King, Zahir Shah, and his entourage on his walls. Two very dirty children came and stared at us. I produced Yahya's letter, which the man made a semblance of reading and understanding (I was not so sure), and then shook his head.

'*Bax ne, bax ne*', he repeated, using the Farsi word which obviously comes from the English. The language barrier effectively prevented any deeper enquiry, so we left just before it got dark.

The walk back turned out to be longer than we anticipated. We missed the turning to the tree and by the time we had discovered our error we had reached Tunkhu, a big village set on the top of a rocky hill. Exhausted, we turned and stumbled back along the path; luckily the moon had risen and shone brilliantly. At around nine we lost our way in a field where some men were threshing, driving their oxen

round and round in a circle over the stalks of wheat. With the
wonderfully spontaneous hospitality that all Afghan countrymen
display, one of them immediately invited us to drink tea and led the
way to his house. We were both so tired now that all we could do was
to sink down on the floor in a kind of stupor. I did, however, manage
to produce the letter. We watched them poring over it in the light of
the one oil lamp without much hope, and sure enough after a few
minutes our host shook his head.

We drank our tea dejectedly and an hour later, just as we were
about to leave, they brought us rice and boiled goat. We were so
exhausted that we could hardly eat. After much handshaking, we
finally set off at around ten and did not reach the tree until nearly
eleven. As we blundered about in the darkness, we thought they had
gone. Then a muffled shout came from the field above and we went
up to find Charles lying in his sleeping bag on a very uneven and
stony piece of ground.

'Christ, where have you been?' he asked, sitting up.

'We got lost, walked as far as Tunkhu and had tea and rice with
some farmer.'

'You're lucky,' Charles said. 'We've had bugger all.'

'Where's Tom?'

'He walked down to the *qarârgâh* to find Yahya. I was getting quite
worried about you, I must admit. Sandy?'

'Yes.'

'I have a confession to make. I smoked one of our last cigars.'

'How the hell?'

'I took it out of your rucksack.'

I quelled an unworthy surge of selfishness.

'I'm sorry,' Charles said. 'It was bloody lonely up here on my
own.'

We unrolled our sleeping bags. Even the extreme discomfort of the
ground could not keep me awake. But only a few hours later, at two,
we were awakened by Tom and a group of mujahideen.

'Tom?'

'What's going on?'

'The Russians are advancing up the Darra. They've taken
Tambonnah. Yahya wants you to move to the *qarârgâh* immediately.
He's worried about us getting cut off.'

There's nothing like the threat of being captured by the Russians
to get you up. The genie performed his daily miracle in record time

and with the muj shouldering our six pieces of equipment, we set off down the path that was now becoming, if not a friend, at least an old acquaintance.

Even with our equipment, the muj went fast and when the moon set, it became doubly difficult. The lead man had a torch and by keeping close to him, I found it just manageable. For one long stretch we had to follow a narrow path beside an irrigation channel, with a steep drop on the left. At one point I slipped and only the thorny bushes saved me. At others we had to jump across the irrigation channel and clamber up steep outcrops of rock. After a forced march of two hours we reached the others, camped out at the foot of some rocks on a patch of sand. Jean-José was sick and Tom had lent him his sleeping bag. Jean-Philippe was wrapped in his *pattu* like a hibernating hedgehog and only Tony, the professional, looked reasonably comfortable. We stretched out for an hour's rest, praising Tom for his heroic effort. If he had not volunteered to walk all the way up to get us, the muj might have taken a long time finding us in the dark and we could have been cut off.

Shortly after dawn the Russians were busy again. We could hear the sound of their advancing gunfire and a couple of helicopters appeared just down the valley. Looking round our position, I saw that there were about fifty mujahideen among the rocks, all well-armed. Yahya appeared.

'Are you ready to leave?'

'Yes, where are we going?'

'Up this valley, the Hazara.' He nodded his head vaguely. 'The Russians are very near. Masud says you must go to a safe place.'

A quarter of a mile up the path, we met Masud himself with his aides coming down at a great pace. We shook hands and I said in French: 'We found some of our equipment in Abdullah Kheil but not the camera. We urgently need the camera. Also, we want to stay here, with you and not go back to Pakistan.' I said this deliberately because Tony had reported Yahya as raising the possibility.

'*Non, non,*' Masud replied immediately. 'You will stay here, but in a safe place higher up the mountain.' Then, addressing Yahya and our veteran mujahid escort, Masud ordered that we were to be well fed, given a clean change of clothes and in general looked after. He spoke with great incisiveness but seemed calm and very much in control. There were absolutely no signs of panic. I could not help being impressed by his concern for us, despite the overriding priority of the Russian offensive. He also passed on the latest military news. The Russians had infiltrated fifty to a hundred airborne 'commandos' over the mountain at Sakh; an attempt to link up with the main armoured push up the Darra, which had now, according to Masud, reached the vicinity of Tambonnah. This pincer movement, if successful, would effectively cut off Tambonnah and suggested that the Russians were using their crack troops to take on the mujahideen at their own game: mountain warfare. This was a new development which could be ominous, despite Masud's air of confidence. He sped off towards the *qarârgâh* and we set off up the Hazara Valley, a vista of idyllic loveliness in the early morning sunshine. Only the beat of the helicopters reminded us that the war was close and getting closer.

8

As we left the wide river bed and started climbing I heard the sound
of helicopters and turned to watch three of them rocket the bottom of
the valley, somewhere near the first *qarârgâh*. They hovered like evil
hawks in the clear air, their double rotors a faint blur, and loosed off
their deadly charges. The streak of smoke from the rockets moved so
fast it almost defeated the eye, and the crack of the explosions drifted
dully up towards us. We turned and tackled the slope. It was hard
going, through meadows bright with blue and yellow Alpine flowers,
the cornflowers looking as if they had been freshly enamelled. We
came to a fork in the valley and climbed left up a very steep slope,
past a mosque and a few houses. After that the rise was more gradual
to the last village, called Sebhá (apple tree in Farsi). After some
shouting between our friendly escort and his neighbours we were led
to the last and highest house where we collapsed on the floor and
promptly went to sleep. We woke to find our host carrying in hot *nan*
and a mound of fresh unsalted butter on which we gorged ourselves.

My watch told me it was 2 September and my diary that this was
the twenty-third day since we had crossed the border and the seventh
day of the Russian offensive.

Despite the long walk of the day before, the disturbed night and
the morning's journey, I was so excited by the discovery of some of
our equipment, which we had left hidden among the rocks at the
second *qarârgâh*, that I was determined not to let the trail go cold.
After some argument with Yahya I finally persuaded him to let us
trek up the Darra again for another search. Tony and Charles said
they would come with me, and Yahya, who I am sure did not fancy
the expedition himself, instructed a young medical assistant called

Mirabuddin to go in his place. He wrote out the obligatory pass-cum-letter and off we went, reaching the *qarârgâh* in under two hours.

The mujahideen were still there, plus a lot of refugees camped out in caves among the rocks. We had a long wait while Mirabuddin tried to find out what was happening. Finally Masud's secretary, a young man with an educated air, came over and sat down on the ground beside us.

Tony explained our predicament and the secretary, after a glance at me, said in Farsi: 'We are very sorry that an old man like him has had to go to all this trouble.'

When Tony translated, tongue in cheek, I became exceedingly angry.

'What the hell's he talking about? Does he think I can't walk up the Darra?'

Tony cut in soothingly, 'It's all right, I've already told him that you could walk him off his feet any day.'

I was mollified but not surprised by the remark. Masud was twenty-eight, the secretary I guessed about twenty-five, and Mirabuddin was a beardless youth of only eighteen, the son of a mullah from the village of Astana. His French was fluent and he was far more mature than anyone of his age I had ever met before. Another piece of paper was added to our collection and, with the sun already declining, we set off along the path we had traversed with such difficulty the night before, reaching the village of Tunkhu, on its outcrop of rock, as darkness fell. While we rested in the middle of the village, Mirabuddin went off to find the headman.

He came back with him a few minutes later, announcing: 'The *malik* says Masud sent sixty men to bring your equipment and the arms from Boularenn. He has the list of all the people who went from this village, about forty persons. And he says they have some of your equipment here.'

Our exhaustion vanished and we scrambled to our feet. The headman led us out of the village and up along the path Nigel and I had twice walked the night before, finally stopping at a farm which looked familiar. He shouted up at a darkened window and eventually a man appeared in the doorway. Despite the poor light I recognized our hospitable unshaven friend from the previous night. After a brief conversation he disappeared, returning a few minutes later with a heavy black metal case. Charles gave a whoop.

'The one hundred and ten!' he shouted joyfully. A second man followed, staggering under the weight of another 110 recorder.

I suddenly became angry at the thought that Nigel and I had been within a few feet of the recorders and the farmer had said not a word.

'Why the hell didn't he tell us he had this equipment when we were here yesterday?' I snapped.

Mirabuddin translated and immediately the farmer's voice rose in matching anger.

'He says he did not know it was yours.'

'But we showed him Yahya's letter saying we were looking for the equipment.'

As the farmer went off into another long tirade, Tony said: 'He can't read, so he didn't know what your letter said. But he knows he's in the wrong and he's trying to cover up his guilt.'

We left the recorders with instructions from the *malik* that they were to be carried down to us next day and tramped on up the valley. It was now getting on for nine, we had not eaten since our bread and butter lunch, and Charles and I in particular were close to exhaustion. We passed the famous tree from where we had watched the bombing and came to the next hamlet, the target of the attack. It still seemed to be more or less intact, a huddle of big fortress-like houses on the edge of a hill overlooking the river. By going to several different houses we discovered the tarpaulin that covered the special saddle and Tony's rucksack, as well as a number of bags of medicines belonging to Jean-Philippe. But no sign of the camera, although we were told it was in a house at the very top of the valley. We crossed the river and made for the commander's house where Charles and I had slept two nights before. He was away – still engaged against the Russians I presumed – so we bedded down on his floor and went to sleep on empty stomachs.

Overnight I had to wrestle with a small devil. Charles and I wanted to carry on to the top of the valley to try to find the camera, but Mirabuddin was anxious to get back: he was after all supposed to be working with Jean-Philippe. I thought of pushing on by ourselves, but without Mirabuddin it would be a waste of time, as the experience with the Tunkhu farmers had shown. We might be in the same house as the camera and never know it. Mirabuddin clinched the argument by assuring us that we now knew the name of the man who had carried the camera from Boularenn and in whose house it now was. It would be a simple matter, he implied, to have it brought down. The final argument, of course, was that the Russians were still

Gulai Dar, the dashing baker turned guerrilla, showing off a captured Russian AGS17 (automatic grenade launcher) above Rokha (previous page)

Boy with a home-made gun. All Afghans grow up with guns and each tribesman has the right to carry arms (left)

Aziz Mohammed, the self-taught gunsmith, who was drawn to the Panjsher by Masud's reputation and stayed on as armourer (above)

'Mine host' at Parende, whose rocket-damaged roof leaked but whose plates of chips put new heart into the expedition (below)

An SU 25, the latest Russian ground attack fighter-bomber, in action over the Panjsher Valley. In 1982 the Russians had a squadron at Bagram, the first seen outside the Soviet Union (top)

SU 25s bombing Abdullah Kheil, a side valley of the Panjsher. The villages and farms were the targets. The intention seemed to be to strike terror into the local population. Charles Morgan stood up to take these pictures while the shrapnel whistled through the branches above our heads (above and right)

Unexploded Russian bombs littered the countryside, not exactly a tribute to the efficiency of the Soviet arms industry

A Russian gasmask, left behind in the Hazara, a side valley of the Panjsher, after the August-September offensive (inset)

Refugee children at Paryan. They lived in a cave with their baby sister. Masud estimated there were 40,000 refugees in the Panjsher (overleaf)

advancing and there was always the chance that we would get cut off. So, reluctantly, I agreed to abandon the search.

We left at four, slithering down the hill past the apricot tree to the river in the dark. As we breasted the slope on the other side the sun was coming up over the mountains of Nuristan, far to the east, and for a time the beauty of the morning banished our hunger and our gloomier thoughts. A brisk walk brought us to the *qarârgâh* among the rocks in time for a breakfast of bread and boiled goat. We were so hungry that we gobbled it down greedily, sitting with our backs to the rock, while a mujahid climbed a big acacia tree and broke off whole branches for firewood. There were thirty or forty fighters there and, given the fact that the Russian offensive was at its height, they seemed in remarkably good nick.

We investigated our growing stock of equipment piled under an overhanging rock and the indispensable Mirabuddin assured us that it would be brought up to Sebhá later in the day. He was clearly anxious to get back, especially so when four helicopters appeared and started rocketing and machine-gunning the mountainside. According to Mirabuddin, they were attacking a group of mujahideen who had pinned down between one and two hundred Russian troops on Sakh mountain. The mujahideen, who were only three hundred yards from the Russians and above them, were planning an assault that night, he said, equipped with two Dashakas and a cannon. If all this were true, the Russians might be in for a rough night. We arrived in Sebhá just in time for a very good lunch of goat and soup. Our immensely helpful farmer-muj was clearly obeying Masud's instructions to the letter.

After our recent exertions, I was grateful to have a rest next day. But I found sitting in the house infinitely depressing so I took my book and radio outside, and was just settling down in a corner of a field when I noticed the ground becoming damp. They had started to irrigate the field and I had not noticed I was sitting beside a miniature channel.

Every now and then a jet would roar overhead, on its way to or from a bombing mission, and refugees continued to trickle up the valley. Yahya and our host were anxious we should not be seen by passers-by; the old worry about Russian spies, and probably well-founded. As we were to discover later, the K.G.B. had helped to set up a sister organization in Afghanistan, called Khad, and was trying hard to infiltrate the Resistance. When, as happened occasionally, people passing did see us, they were so taken aback to find foreigners in this remote spot that they stared at us with embarrassing intensity.

I had brought two tapes with me, Mozart's *Marriage of Figaro* and Mahler's *Fourth Symphony*, and after lunch I listened to the Mahler for the first time. I was stunned by its lyricism and concluded that he must have been in love when he wrote it. There is in particular a very romantic and tender theme which struck me as being quintessentially German. Jean-Philippe begged to be allowed to hear it too and spent a happy hour, curled up like a hedgehog with the earphones on. It was an unusually intellectual day all round. I also started mapping out the plot for a thriller involving an attack on the Salang Tunnel, built by the Russians in 1964. It runs for almost two miles through the Hindu Kush, a strategic link in the Russian supply line from the border to Kabul. Obviously its destruction would be a tremendous coup for the mujahideen.

I noted in my diary, as a matter of some moment, that thanks to Yahya's influence on the commissariat, we had chicken for dinner. But the promised arrival of the equipment from the *qarârgâh* did not materialize.

Sunday, 5 September, brought only bad news. It was exactly five weeks since we had left London and hardly a foot of the programme was shot. That was bad enough, but we now heard that the Russians were still advancing and that the *qarârgâh* had been evacuated. I said a small prayer that our gear had been moved to safety and decided to make one more attempt to find the camera. Charles, Mirabuddin and I set off at four. About half-way to the *qarârgâh* we came on a group of mujahideen under Sharia, one of Masud's lieutenants; a diminutive man with tiny hands and a reedy voice who came from the north, from Mazar-i-Sharif or Kunduz, and who seemed quite unfitted for the rough and tumble of guerrilla warfare. He described himself as the cultural officer but I put him down as a political commissar.

We accompanied them down the mountain, reaching the river just after six. There they stopped to wash and pray, spreading their *pattus* on the stones in the middle of the dry river bed and facing towards Mecca. As the level sun gilded the mountains, softening their harshness and making shadow pools of purple, they chanted '*Allah o Akbar, Allah o Akbar*' (God is great) and knelt to touch their foreheads on the pale stones. A bomb had ripped a great chunk of the river bank away, scattering rocks and earth over a wide area only a hundred yards from a big house that looked like a beige fort, set on a headland where the Hazara meets the Darra. While he waited for orders, Sharia and I had a long talk about Masud and the Resistance. In reply to my question, he said that he saw no reason why Masud should not become a national leader, claiming it made no difference that he was a Tadjik, a member of a minority group, and not a Pathan. I doubted if he was right but the important thing, it seemed to me, was that they were clearly thinking in these terms. People from all over Afghanistan made the journey to the Panjsher to seek Masud's help, he said.

With the wind becoming chilly and a lack of any positive orders, Sharia decided we should climb up to the village above us and have something to eat. By now Charles and I were desperately tired but we struggled up the hill and did justice to a big bowl of yoghurt.

The news from the front continued to be bad; the Russians were still advancing and Sharia was anxious for us to head up the Hazara. But this would have meant abandoning our personal kit and I refused. So we set off for Sebhá, but by now it was so late that when we reached the little mosque at the top of its steep slope, Mirabuddin proposed spending the night there. We got to bed at one, unrolling our sleeping bags in the clean hay which covered the floor. We were up at five and once again the beauty of the morning was so magical that for a short time I forgot our problems. We reached Sebhá at around seven to find Yahya in a state of some excitement. He had received a message from Masud instructing us all to go up the Hazara Valley to a village called Astana. We looked at one another with long faces. It sounded like the beginning of the end. If we went any further, we would be out of the Panjsher.

Yahya wanted us to leave at once so we repacked our kitbags, taking only essentials. An argument ensued as to whether Mr Knorr's soups came into that category, with two of us insisting that they did and two being against carrying any extra weight. We snarled at one another like dogs fighting over a bone: the idea of a defeat, both military and personal, was sapping our energies and our tempers. It did not occur to me at the time that on top of all our troubles, the altitude was also taking its toll – Sebhá must have been around ten thousand feet.

Having stacked all our equipment on the landing at the top of the stairs, we set off down the stony track, passing odd groups of refugees coming in the opposite direction, their animals loaded with their household goods. Occasionally we would pass a man on horseback with his wife riding pillion, robed from head to foot in a *chadary*. She could see out through a sort of lattice window but nobody could see her. The women rarely spoke but no man ever passed by in silence. Greetings were always exchanged and hands were usually shaken, the other travellers staring in unfeigned astonishment at the sight of half a dozen foreigners suddenly emerging round the side of a mountain. Once we met a whole string of mujahideen travelling in the opposite direction. There must have been thirty or forty of them and they stopped at the side of the path while each of them shook each of us by the hand as we passed. It was no perfunctory handshake, they wanted to welcome us as kindred spirits, and brothers-in-arms.

As we descended, I realized that this might be our last chance of recovering the missing camera and that, since we could not get to Abdullah Kheïl by the customary route, we would have to go over the mountain, although the way looked horribly steep. Yahya did not like the idea. As far as he was concerned Masud had given his instructions and that was that – they carried the force of a military order. It would be a very brave or very foolish man who ignored them. The four of us had gone on ahead and when we came to the river we crossed to the west bank, jumping from stone to stone. It was only some time later that I noticed that Yahya, Tony, Jean-Philippe and Jean-José had stayed on the far bank. Mirabuddin came hurrying along to catch us up.

'Yahya wants you to go back to the other side. He says we must go up the Hazara. The Russians are still advancing.'

I repeated our determination to make one last try to find the camera by climbing over the intervening ridge into the Darra.

'We would be very grateful if you would come with us.'

Mirabuddin shook his head. 'I can't leave Jean-Philippe. I must translate for him when he sees patients. But I will tell Yahya that he must go with you over the mountain to Abdullah Kheil.' With that he scrambled off down the precipitous slope to the river. We sat waiting in the sunshine, enjoying the sights and sounds of a summer morning in the high mountains. Bees worked single-mindedly among the Alpine flowers, sprouting so miraculously from the parched earth, and restless brown fritillaries swerved among the dog roses and camel thorn. Hawks sailed past on stiff wings and below us the rush of the river was muted to a distant song. We could see the others, tiny figures against the sweep of the valley, plodding along the far bank.

After ten minutes Mirabuddin emerged from the cliff below and crossed the river. He and the others vanished among some trees and then, to our surprise, Mirabuddin reappeared, crossed the river again, and came up the hill towards us. Sweating from his climb, he recounted that Yahya, obviously reluctant to countermand his brother's orders, had refused to come with us. He had made all sorts of excuses, saying he did not know where Masud was, where the camera was, or the way over the mountain to Abdullah Kheil. Instead, he had sent Mirabuddin back to look after us. For that I was grateful since, apart from his skill as an interpreter, he was intelligent and extremely likeable.

We climbed on up to the village, called Khodjeghar, finishing up in the mosque which bore the scars of a Russian rocket attack.

In these villages, mosques are used as places to rest and congregate as well as to pray. Several mujahideen who had been asleep on the floor got up as soon as we walked in: one was a tall, devil-may-care machine gunner who was full of stirring tales. After lunch I watched the local farmers winnowing wheat by hand, tossing the grain in the air with flat wooden shovels. The ripe ears fall straight to the ground but the chaff, being lighter, is blown by the wind and falls separately. With the jagged brown peaks behind the winnowers sharp against the immaculate blue sky, the beauty and simplicity of the scene made me think of the Old Testament.

Mirabuddin had been questioning the locals about the *direttissima* route to Abdullah Kheil and my heart sank as I examined it. We would have to climb to just below the crest of a high, jagged ridge, and then clamber up a gully to a high col. It looked so formidable that our morale sank accordingly, only reviving with the arrival of a bright friendly newcomer called Abdul Hai, whom Mirabuddin introduced as Masud's assistant. We immediately outlined our problem to him. Could we go over the mountain to Abdullah Kheil? To my considerable surprise, he nodded.

'Yes, you can cross the mountain to Abdullah Kheil but it will be hard!' I did not entirely believe that he would let us try.

'When can we go?'

'Tonight.' We had not expected this and it rather floored us. Someone complained of being too tired. It would be sensible to have a rest before tackling what would assuredly be an exhausting climb.

'Tomorrow,' I said, 'we'd like to go tomorrow. But we'll need six porters to carry the equipment.'

Abdul Hai nodded. 'Yes, that's all right.'

I thanked him effusively but somehow doubted if they would ever materialize. Abdul Hai's manner was extremely cheerful and we now found out why. He announced that the front was stabilizing and that things should get easier. Before going to bed, we had a long talk about our film and the possible repercussions it would have for the Resistance. I rather liked him – he was excessively polite and helpful, though Nigel thought he was unreliable and insincere.

In the morning, while the jovial machine gunner prepared to depart for the mountains, we were taken to the top of the village and shown into a tiny, ice-cold cave. Apart from it being too small to hold all of us, I was so frozen after five minutes that I insisted on sitting outside in the morning sunshine, ignoring the repeated attempts of the Afghans to make us take cover.

'Bam, bam. Russ bam,' they kept saying, pointing to the sky every time we heard the noise of an aircraft.

I became so irritated by their refrain that I shouted back, 'Don't be bloody silly, it's miles away and it couldn't possibly see us anyway.'

The Antonov reconnaissance planes worried them most and, while we may have been over-contemptuous of Russian capabilities, the Afghans went to the other extreme. To add to our frustrations, we now heard that Abdul Hai had sent a message by runner to Masud, asking permission for us to go to Abdullah Kheil. Even as Masud's number two, he was unable to authorize our journey. Late in the day, the messenger returned saying that when he reached the top of the ridge he had seen flares and, believing the Russians were close, had turned back.

I was trying to read, although constantly distracted by the apparently insoluble problem of the camera, when the jets appeared and started bombing Abdullah Kheil. They came in high over our valley and then dived steeply, disappearing behind the ridge to bomb. Muffled explosions reverberated as the jets climbed up into the azure sky on the far side of the valley, circled and came back again. The bombing of Abdullah Kheil went on all morning while, fifty yards below us, the villagers calmly killed a cow, the crimson blood running across the hard ground beneath the mulberry trees and into the wheatfield below. They hacked the carcase into joints and carried them off in triumph to their houses.

Nothing daunted by the gory scene, we followed the call for lunch with our usual alacrity. We started with some of Mr Knorr's delicacies, followed by chicken, as a special treat, although as usual there was not enough. After lunch we returned to our hillside and listened to the Antonov droning above us, working over the ground like a pointer, informing the jets of the result of their strikes and calling up new targets. Around four, we heard gunfire, possibly heavy mortars, from Abdullah Kheil. As the sun went down I noticed an autumnal chill in the wind for the first time, and watched a few yellow leaves detach themselves from the walnut and apricot trees and float gently to the ground. The sun vanished from the valley as if a curtain had dropped and I experienced a sense of melancholy which deepened with every leaf that fell.

Earlier in the day, Nigel and I had sat on a big rock in the sunshine talking frankly and rationally about our predicament. We both agreed that we were running out of time, even if we found the camera the next day; and given that day's bombing, that was extremely unlikely. At best, we would have a struggle to gather enough material for a one-hour documentary: at worst, we might not have a programme at all.

I said: 'It was my idea to come to Afghanistan, it's my responsibility that we're here and so I must take the blame.' Tom, who was sitting reading below, heard me and came climbing up.

'You mustn't say that, Sandy. It's not your fault at all,' he said with enormous sympathy. I felt very touched by this show of solidarity. He had also overheard me say that we would have to leave by the 24th, less than three weeks away, so that we could be back in London by the middle of October. Even then, we would be two weeks behind schedule and that meant several thousand pounds on the budget. But even that was being optimistic. It might take another week or even ten days to track down the camera, which would take us to, say, 17 September. We would never be able to film a one-hour documentary in a week: it would take us at least a fortnight, so the 24 October deadline was totally unrealistic. We would be lucky if we had completed our filming by the end of September.

It was in a mood of mounting depression that we returned to the mosque. For once, the beauty of the mountains in the evening light failed to move me. But worse was to follow.

9

I woke at two to find everyone up. We had to leave immediately, Mirabuddin said, because the situation had become too dangerous (a complete volte-face from the previous night); there were no mujahideen to defend us and the village was short of food. On the far side of the big room Nigel and Charles were already deep in conversation with Abdul Hai. I listened without enthusiasm as he explained that there was now no possibility of trying to reach Abdullah Kheil. The previous evening he had despatched two more mujahideen with a message for Masud but, on reaching the top of the ridge, they had seen houses burning in the valley below, including the *malik*'s where we had stayed, and presuming Russian troops were in occupation, they had turned back. One mujahid said they had seen helicopters rocketing the valley further up and it occurred to me that the houses could have been set on fire by the helicopters or the bombing – and not necessarily by troops on the ground. Whatever the explanation, they had failed to reach Masud who, as it turned out later, was miles away on the other side of the valley. I could find no answer to Abdul Hai's litany of disaster: I had neither the energy nor the arguments to counter it.

Defeated, we left the house at around four, walking down the now familiar path and picking our way across the wide rock-strewn river bed that looked like the surface of the moon. On the far side, a shaky wooden bridge spanned the narrow but fast-flowing Hazara and we turned east into the dawn.

As the sun came up, the high ranges in front of us towards Nuristan stood out sharp and jagged; a grandiose setting for heroic events and a warning of how ruthlessly Afghanistan would punish any weakness. But as the sun climbed higher, reaching down into the narrow valley and burnishing the greens and golds of the meadows and cornfields, the enchanting beauty of the Hazara unfolded itself. We stopped briefly for the mujahideen to wash and pray and went on, climbing slowly.

We made a longish stop for tea at one village and then, at around 11.30, after seven hours' walking we rounded a bend and found ourselves looking down on a pretty village set among huge boulders. Here, where a brawling stream met the Hazara at right angles, was Astana. We crossed the river by stepping stones and stopped at almost the first house, where Yahya and the others turned out to be staying. It was built in the traditional pattern: entrance hall-cum-stable for the animals, a mud staircase to the first floor where there were several rooms, including the kitchen with an open fire in the corner, and the 'front' room, innocent of furniture except for a carpet or two on the floor and cushions and rugs in the corner. There was the odd poster or photograph on the wall, but no books: I hardly saw a book the whole time we were in the Panjsher.

Before lunch I sat by the river and watched wagtails – yellow and either white or pied, they are very similar – flitting from rock to rock in the sunshine. They are wonderfully graceful with their undulating flight, a series of half-loops, and they have a sharp, haunting cry that cuts in above the rush of the river, like a solo violin above the rumble of the orchestra.

Later I moved to the threshing floor, a circular piece of earth, trodden hard, near the river on the other side of the village, and watched the young men bringing in the sheaves, bending under a load twice as high as themselves. Other men were bagging the winnowed grain and carrying it away. They were amazingly strong. One would sit on the ground with his back to the full bag, rope it firmly to himself and then, with little or no help, draw his heels under him and hoist himself and the bag of grain, weighing at a guess at least a hundredweight, straight off the ground. Some could do it without using their hands to push off, purely by thigh power.

A toothless old man with a humorous eye came and sat beside me and tried to engage me in conversation. But once I had explained, 'Doctor né. Journalist. Englestan,' my conversational powers were exhausted. He and various other village worthies had congregated to keep an eye on this vitally important climax to the harvest. As we sat enjoying the warmth of the afternoon sun, a young woman came walking back from the river with a pile of washing, a yellow plastic water bottle at her side and, even more incongruous, a rifle on her shoulder. As I strolled to the house I passed the prettiest woman I had seen in Afghanistan. She carried a tiny, round-eyed, round-faced baby on her back, and led another little girl, in pigtails and pink plastic gumboots, by the hand. She smiled and greeted me, '*Salaam Aleikum.*'

It was the first time a young woman had spoken to me for a month and I felt ridiculously pleased. She had a slightly Chinese or Mongoloid look about her, which meant she was probably Uzbek and might account for her unusual friendliness.

Despite the primitive beauty of our surroundings I could not shake off a deep feeling of failure. I wrote in my diary:

We have now abandoned nearly all the equipment. I feel very sad. It was my idea and I carry the can. The Russian offensive came just too soon, or we came too late: we were far too heavily weighed down: ENG [video tape] is really not right for this sort of very cruel terrain. I am not heartbroken but extremely sad. It is such a waste of time (no, not for me personally), of money and effort, and such a wasted opportunity to make a really first-class film about what is happening here – the unlovely face of Russia's war to smash the Afghan Resistance and enfold the country firmly in the grasp of the S.U. – and the heroic face of the Resistance. Their courage is terrific. The morale of the muj seems unshakable. But how long can the valley survive this sort of pounding?

That night we had a long talk with Yahya. It was the gloomiest review of our prospects so far. He was waiting for his final instructions from Masud, he said, but if the Russian advance continued, we would have to leave the Panjsher and move to another valley on the way to Pakistan.

'Pakistan?' I exclaimed, horrified. 'If we go to Pakistan, we'll never come back. That means abandoning the film and the equipment.'

'We can do two things,' Yahya went on. I tried to concentrate on his good eye and not the one that strayed. 'We can go to Paryan [at the head of the Panjsher Valley and one of the routes to Nuristan] or we can go up this valley here.' He meant the brawling tributary.

'Paryan is better for horses. We can hire horses there,' Yahya continued.

'Can't we get horses from here?' someone asked.

'No, we have to climb a high pass to get to Paryan. At Paryan we can get horses.'

It did not really matter, because we had left our equipment scattered at various points in the Panjsher – the camera, of course, was still missing – and we had only our personal rucksacks with us. After Yahya had finished his tactical appreciation and gone off to organize supper, we went back over the by-now depressingly familiar ground.

'That's it, then,' Tom opined.

'If we go to whatever this place is called, half-way to Pakistan, that's the end of the expedition,' Nigel agreed. He sat like the rest of us, on the floor, reclining against an overstuffed cushion in the dusty cramped room. Like myself, he had several days' stubble on his chin. Lean at the best of times, he had become alarmingly thin. He had caught my cold and now had a hacking cough which the dust seemed to aggravate. I worried about him increasingly because our bag of medicines had gone missing with the camera and he badly needed a course of antibiotics. Charles seemed to suffer continually from diarrhoea, the scourge of Afghanistan, but Tom, after his poor start, was now probably the fittest and strongest. I had lost a lot of weight but felt physically well.

We contemplated the failure of our expedition with a sort of weary resignation. The only saving grace was that it was not really our fault. We could argue endlessly about whether we should have left all the equipment at Boularenn, about the wisdom of using video (instead of film), but, leaving these questions aside, it was an incalculable factor – the Russian offensive – which had brought us to the brink of disaster. I contemplated the prospect of failure with intense distaste, but without any idea of how to avoid it. Instead, I started to rehearse my *mea culpa* to Charles Denton of Central Television, who had sponsored our trip.

At 6.30 the following morning, Thursday, 9 September, the thirtieth day since we crossed the border, an extraordinary thing happened. We were gloomily waiting for breakfast, all the previous night's cares still upon us, when a man arrived with an urgent note from Abdul Hai. 'Do not leave. The Russians have withdrawn. Please come back.' I was immediately enormously excited, although Nigel was much more cautious, sceptical even. A few minutes later Yahya, who was sleeping in another house, came through the doorway and said he was sure it was true. After thirteen days, the

Russians had started to withdraw. We ate our breakfast *nan* and drank our milk tea with a new relish. Immediately afterwards Yahya said he was leaving for the *qarârgâh* to confirm the good news and would send word back as soon as possible for us to follow. Tom immediately said he would go too and I, of course, agreed. Tom was always keen to strike out on his own – he has an independent Irish spirit, despite being born in London – and he liked nothing more than being what the Americans in Vietnam used to call 'point' man; the man at the front.

I was still busy trying to adjust my thoughts to this new development, so totally unexpected, when another message arrived, this time in French: 'To my dear friends, the British journalists. All your equipment has been collected together, but unfortunately the two black cases [the BVU 110s] have been lost and the camera has been totally destroyed in an air raid. With much regret, Masud.' I felt a tremendous sense of despair come over me. I sat on the floor helplessly, not knowing what to do, when Mirabuddin started to giggle behind his hand. I looked up to find him and Jean-Philippe smirking at one another. Slowly, it dawned on me that this was supposed to be a joke. I just managed to stop myself exploding with anger at such a cruel and silly trick and then we all gave a wry laugh. To celebrate, I smoked my last panatella, deriving disproportionate enjoyment from such a small luxury.

Nigel and I strolled up the river and found a meadow where we could half strip, wash and sit in the sun, our ears full of the rush of water and the shrill calls of the wagtails. Even the arrival of some village youths, who stared at us with unnerving intensity, could not entirely upset us, although Nigel grumbled: 'There's absolutely no such thing as privacy in Afghanistan. It simply doesn't exist. Go away, you bloody people!'

Charles arrived to announce triumphantly that he had collected twenty-two eggs from various sources. Lunch of bread and mutton was already arranged, so we ate them in a runny omelette with chopped onion tops. They were delicious and I felt full for the first time in a month.

In the evening, a message arrived from Tom to say that the Russians had indeed gone from the *qarârgâh* and that we should follow as fast as possible. It also included authority for four porters, and ended with the information that he intended to go to Abdullah Kheil to make another attempt to find the camera and recover the

110s. I put down his note feeling tremendously excited and with a new sense of purpose and hope. I wrote in my diary 'Black despair has lifted.' Victory might yet be snatched from the very muzzles of the Russians' guns.

We started the next day well, breakfasting off the remains of Charles's eggs, but the porters took a long time to assemble and we did not leave until nearly ten, making slow progress. Infuriatingly, none of the porters wanted to travel further than the next village and we had to stop three times to recruit new ones. This was not easy, Mirabuddin not having enough clout to get it done quickly.

We reached the bridge over the Hazara by evening and climbed up to a big house perched on a rock. As we laboured up the last steep section, a voice floated down accusingly: 'Where've you been, all this time?' We craned our necks, to see Tom sitting in a window right above us. He came clattering down and led us upstairs, explaining that the mujahideen had not wanted him to go to Abdullah Kheil but had sent messengers instead. He was cheerful and seemed to have everything under control, promising to arrange tea for us in a few minutes. I admired the way in which he made himself so quickly at home in new surroundings and he spoke of the local Commander as if he were an old friend. The latter arrived shortly afterwards, a large, bearded, extremely ebullient fellow who addressed us at the top of his voice.

An hour later, we were taken across the shaky wooden bridge over the moon-like boulders, up the opposite bank and then along the hillside to another house where Yahya, Abdul Hai and a group of mujahideen were ensconced. They rose with smiles of welcome, shook hands and made us sit down, pushing cushions behind our backs. Abdul Hai, with Yahya translating, made a flowery speech of regret for all the hardships and 'troubles' we had suffered and expressed the hope that the rest of our stay would be successful. All our equipment, he said, would be brought to a house a few hundred yards away, which we would make our base; and he promised that the blessed camera, around which every conversation sooner or later revolved, would be tracked down and delivered into our possession with the utmost despatch. Thus spake the pleasantly smiling Abdul Hai. I was much more inclined to take him at his word than Nigel, who remained throughout highly sceptical of his promises and irritated by his somewhat unctuous manner; but even I was cautious in my diary that night, commenting 'We'll see.'

When I quizzed Abdul Hai about the reasons for the Russian withdrawal, he answered with a confidence that reminded me of a politician.

'The Russians thought that the mujahideen were demoralized after the first offensive [May-July]. They thought we would surrender and lay down our arms and that the local people would flock to the Government. When they discovered that the people did not turn to the Government forces and that the mujahideen were still ready to fight, they gave up and withdrew.'

Possible, I supposed, but not probable. I thought it more likely that the Russians had made merely a tactical withdrawal and that we had not heard the last of them. When we left to walk back to our new house, we could see flashes of gunfire from the bottom of the valley, and a few seconds later heard the rumble of the explosions.

Next morning, the jets were abroad early, their sudden roar shattering the limpid calm. Our new house was devoid of furniture and even cooking utensils. After breakfast I climbed up to the flat roof, where apricots were spread out to dry, and spent most of the morning writing a script. For the first time, cloud covered the valley, signalling that autumn was on the way: a worrying thought, given that we had not even started to make our film, let alone plan our departure. The accursed Antonov was active, droning malevolently above me, and from far down the valley I could hear the sound of bombing.

Next morning I read the draft script to Nigel and Charles in turn, and both approved with only one or two minor criticisms. They may, of course, have felt it was an exercise in futility: the chances of our making a successful documentary seemed to be diminishing with each day that went past.

Later, after I had been up the mountain to commune with nature, I was strolling towards the next group of houses when two jets went hurtling high overhead. Seconds later I heard several explosions about four or five miles away – I guessed at Jerali. Dust and smoke rose lazily in the air and the echoes of the bombing reverberated off the mountains opposite like thunder. I wondered why the Russians should attack a little place like Jerali with no obvious military significance, and concluded that it was another exercise in terror.

I had my notebook with me and, with time hanging heavy on my hands, I started to sketch the fortress-like houses on the river bank opposite. The design was so complicated that I abandoned my first

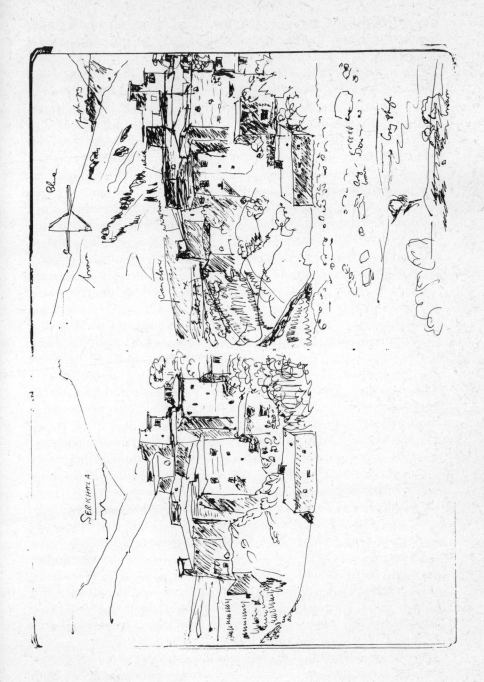

attempt, but the second was passable. A man came and looked over my shoulder and made encouraging noises, telling me that the village or hamlet was called Serkhala.

I returned to find the others sleeping or reading. Dinner was awful – rice and a small amount of stringy goat. 'I thought they promised us good food and plenty of it,' Nigel complained. He was right. Yahya, quoting Abdul Hai, had told us on the night we arrived that every effort would be made to give us better food. Nigel, in particular, complained repeatedly about feeling weak and was still racked by a terrible cough. Sometimes, hearing him cough and looking at his haggard face, I wondered if he would have the strength to survive. Out of pride he had not asked Jean-Philippe for help and our medicines were still missing. Tom and Charles seemed to be able to force down fair amounts of rice, but Nigel was eating almost nothing: both he and I found the rice so tasteless that it was difficult to swallow enough to keep our strength up. On the rare occasions I saw myself in a mirror, I realized that I had become unattractively skinny.

The next day, Nigel and I crossed the river after breakfast and walked a mile or so downstream to the house where Abdul Hai had taken up residence. We followed an irrigation channel, cleverly cut into the hillside, the water as clear, fast-running and cold as a Highland burn. Men and women were harvesting in the tiny fields beside the river, the women's dresses making bright spots of colour against the stubble, like figures in a Corot landscape.

Abdul Hai was holding court in a large airy room overlooking the river. As we were ushered in, he rose with his customary mannerly smile. A row of moustachioed, turbaned figures sitting against the wall greeted us gravely. Most of them were from the north, from Badakhshan, also Tadjiks and supporters of the Masud cause.

We told Abdul Hai we were getting desperate and that if he could not find the camera for us, we would go back to Abdullah Kheil ourselves. He was against that, and immediately wrote out another note and sent it off with a messenger. He begged us to be patient, saying they were doing everything possible to find the camera and bring it to us. He rose smilingly to bid us farewell. As we walked back, Nigel said, 'I don't trust him. He promises everything and does nothing. He's full of piss and wind.'

I was more forgiving than Nigel, and was prepared to believe that Abdul Hai was doing his best, however inadequate it might be. Both

of us, of course, were becoming increasingly doubtful that we would
ever find the camera again.

While Nigel climbed up the hill to our house, I crossed the great
boulders of the river bed to where the Hazara had been dammed to
make a small blue-green lake. It lay unruffled and somewhat
mysterious in the sunshine (the clouds had vanished) and I half
expected an arm to rise from the centre of the lake and brandish, if
not Excalibur, at least our Ikegami camera. At the near end, where a
little stream flowed in, hundreds of small fish basked in the shallows
and I thought that if only we had a net we could supplement our
meagre diet. I strolled on, putting up a kite or buzzard which planed
majestically across the water, disappearing behind a small rocky
bluff. A hundred yards further on, a kingfisher, which had been
sitting motionless on a dead stump sticking out of the water, made a
tantalizingly swift blue flash.

My nature ramble was brutally disturbed. Two jets, high in the
blue, screamed across the sky in an almost identical flight pattern to
the previous day and dropped three or four bombs on Jerali. I
wondered anxiously about Jean-Philippe and Mirabuddin, who had
gone up early to treat casualties from the previous day's bombing. As
I walked back to the house, I watched the grey-brown cloud of smoke
and dust hanging in the still air of the valley.

That night a note arrived from Abdul Hai:

To dear houst Mr Sandy!
and other gentel companiones!
pleas accept my greeting
I send again the Mudir
Shamsoddin to providing
your residual instrumentes.
By honour
[signed] Abdul Hai

At least he was trying.

The following day seemed to pass extremely slowly. Charles and I
went down to the lake to see if we could catch some tiddlers for lunch:
we thought they might taste a bit like whitebait. We borrowed
Nigel's mosquito net, which was about two feet across at the mouth
and three or four feet long, and I thought if we could prop it open,
bait it and then tug it shut, we might catch something. As soon as the
tiddlers saw us they darted off at high speed and the net proved

extremely difficult to prop open. We managed it eventually but when, after half an hour or so of bathing our feet and lying in the sun, we crept back to the scene of operations, hardly any fish had entered into the spirit of the thing. On my direction, Charles tugged the bright blue nylon cord to close the net, we rushed forward expectantly. But to our disappointment we found we had netted only one small sprat. We bore it back to the house, where Nigel was unimpressed.

'I hope you'll wash out my mosquito net when you've finished with it,' he said and settled down to his rice.

The afternoon of our thirty-fifth day in Afghanistan was drifting away towards sunset and oblivion, when I heard a commotion on the stairs. I was sitting on the floor, my back to the wall, reading the second half of *Vanity Fair*. (I had torn the book in half so that Nigel could read the first part.) I put down the book and glanced through the half-open door to see a stalwart farmer clumping past, carrying something heavy. A second appeared, bent under a big black box. Then a third farmer came into view and I caught sight of the shiny metal box which contained the camera. Very excited, I got to my feet shouting, 'Hey, the camera's arrived and the BVUs'. We were all on our feet now and crowding through the doorway into the corridor. The three farmers dropped their loads, wiped the sweat from their faces and straightened their backs. Even for them it must have been an exhausting journey of ten or fifteen miles over rough ground and, while the BVUs were heavier, the sharp-edged camera box must have been extremely awkward to carry. We shook the porters warmly by the hand, but there was only one thought in our minds. Was the camera working? After a brief, increasingly excited examination, it seemed that the answer was yes! I could hardly contain myself. Tom said he would have to carry out a proper test, but it looked as if, after all the anguish of the past days and weeks, we would be able to start shooting. My prayers had worked.

I put in my diary that night: '5 p.m. Tremendous excitement. The camera has finally arrived. Plus the two 110s. Three v. stout farmers all the way from Abdullah Kheil. What extraordinary euphoria. We can start at last.'

10

We started filming after breakfast on 15 September, our thirty-sixth day in Afghanistan. Curiously, the long frustrating period of waiting had had an unexpected effect and instead of everyone being mad keen to start, there was a distinct mood of reluctance, which I put down to mental and physical exhaustion. It was as if, having abandoned the project in our minds, we found it required a superhuman effort to reverse our ideas, rather like stopping a supertanker at full speed. Tom seemed to be particularly unhappy and even Charles was less than enthusiastic, maybe because he was still having trouble with his insides; there is nothing more debilitating and depressing than constant diarrhoea.

However, we set up the camera on the roof, from which we had a superb view up and down the valley. At one end a terraced patchwork of green-gold fields caught the morning sun, the altitude and distance giving them the magical, remote quality of a Shangri-La. After half an hour of filming, we dismantled the gear and with Charles shouldering the camera, Tom the recorder and myself the tripod, crossed the river to the *qarârgâh* opposite.

We were now joined by a young French student, Stéphane, who arrived with two new doctors. Stéphane's father had served as a diplomat in Kabul, and so he was brought up there and had learned Farsi. He was doubly welcome: he had brought in with him £20,000-worth of Afghanis collected in France for Masud; while his fluency in Farsi made him valuable to us.

Stéphane had been told by Masud that the Russians were planting mines timed to go off after a fortnight releasing some sort of gas.

Everyone had been warned to be on the lookout, but nobody, including Masud, knew if there was any truth in the story. Tom had discovered the day before that the mujahideen had found a Russian gasmask, and I wanted to use it in the film to demonstrate the possible use of gas by the Russians – though whether it was 'stun' gas or something more lethal, it was obviously impossible to say. It was only later, when I learned that all Russian soldiers carry gas masks as part of their regular equipment, that I realized the argument to be specious and cut the reference out of the film.

Stéphane had picked up a small, khaki-coloured anti-personnel mine (after exploding it with a stone) on a mountain pass and presented me with it. You could see from what was left that it had been heart-shaped, although anything more hideously inhuman and heartless would have been hard to imagine. The Russians apparently scattered them from helicopters and they lay, looking harmless enough, waiting to blow off the hand or foot of an unsuspecting Afghan: children, herding the family flocks of sheep and goats, were the chief victims, we were told. It made my blood boil to think of some innocent child stepping on one of these evil devices, or worse still, attracted by a novel shape among the stones of the hillside, bending down to pick it up.

Yahya said Abdul Hai wanted to see me, so after we had finished filming, and while the others crossed the river to shoot some harvesting scenes, Yahya and I followed the irrigation channel to his house. Abdul Hai, full of smiles, was just sitting down to lunch and invited us to join him. It was a delicious meal of fresh, hot bread, yoghurt and grapes, but I could not help feeling guilty as I ate, conscious that the others would be having the usual tough and tasteless goat and rice. Abdul Hai had promised several times to provide us with better fare but so far nothing had happened.

After lunch, while we sipped our tea, I produced a piece of paper with a list of items we wanted to film. To my surprise and annoyance, Abdul Hai upstaged me by also producing a list and reading it out. For a moment I was cross, but then I saw the funny side, particularly as it turned out that his list was almost identical to mine. We were both agreed on the need to film the mujahideen at prayer and Abdul Hai promised that a mullah would come up to our house that afternoon to organize the meeting. We discussed filming a school with children singing the party song, but because of the two offensives and the bombing, classes had been in abeyance for most of the summer and it looked as if it would be difficult to organize. As we talked, I began to think the best thing would be to head down the main valley, both to make contact with Masud as soon as possible and to film any military activity that might still be in progress. We did not know how far the Russians had withdrawn – whether they were still in Rokha or had left the valley entirely.

Yahya and I walked back up the hill to find the others stretched out in our room, having had a miserable lunch. When I had to confess how well we had fared, there was a splutter of anger from Nigel.

'Did you tell Abdul Hai that while he's eating fresh *mast*, we're still getting the same filthy goat? I never liked or trusted that man. He keeps saying he's sent money to buy food for us but the man here says he hasn't seen a penny. Did you tell him that?' Nigel wanted to know. I had to admit rather lamely that I had not.

'Mr Abdul Hai's full of bullshit,' Nigel concluded crossly. 'That's what he is. Full of bullshit. If we don't get better food we'll never be able to make the journey out. And we've got to make a documentary as well.' The reproach was justified, for Nigel was thinner than ever and seemed to be losing strength rapidly, although his cough was less convulsive.

Charles reported that he and Tom had filmed some men winnowing wheat and a woman husking maize before lunch. As the woman sat in the field in her red dress, with her two young children beside her, an Antonov had flown overhead, its insistent drone imparting a note of menace to the pastoral scene. Charles said he was pleased with the pictures.

Shortly afterwards the mullah, a tall, solemn-looking man with a wispy grey beard, and Abdul Hai arrived with a group of mujahideen for the prayer sequence. No Afghan seems to walk a hundred yards if he can walk a mile and now, lugging the camera and recorder by turns, we followed the mujahideen across the boulder-strewn river bed, past the fortress-like hamlet on the headland, and slowly made our way up the slope beyond. Boys and men from the village followed to see the fun. I kept expecting Abdul Hai to stop but he climbed on, a hundred yards or more in front, finally disappearing over the skyline. It was a beautiful sunny afternoon, the sky a deep azure, with a brisk wind making the foliage of the mulberry trees whirl in a silvery dance. When we finally breasted the slope, we found the mujahideen waiting for us on a little plateau covered with brilliant emerald-green clover. Beyond, the mountains made an imposingly rugged backcloth. Tom however, was not happy about the wind, which was whipping over the exposed plateau with a velocity that would make recording exceedingly tricky. We spent some time trying to find a spot where there was some shelter, but the mullah was eager to start. Muslim prayers are timed to coincide with various periods of the day: this prayer marked the end of the working day and the mujahideen were forming up in two lines, anxious to get on with it. The tall mullah, his grey beard fluttering in the breeze, drew out his compass and consulted it attentively. He was establishing the exact direction of Mecca, the Holy City in Saudi Arabia towards which all Muslims turn to pray five times a day. I reflected that it seemed to be rather a one-way business. The prayers of the Afghan mujahideen flowed ceaselessly over the ocean and the desert towards Mecca, but not much succour in the form of arms or aid seemed to come back. Having established his bearing, the mullah pocketed the compass and indicated his intended stance. Abdul Hai, with his habitual smile, explained that we were a little too close and would we mind moving the camera back a few feet. Charles swore but complied and lay down to shoot from as low an angle as possible. The mullah stepped in front of the two lines of mujahideen, mostly young men in their late teens or early twenties. In front of him was arranged a neat pile of weapons, grouped round the pineapple-shaped rocket of an RPG. The mujahideen always placed their weapons on the ground in front of them when they prayed, but I noticed that when the camera was in evidence, they always managed things just a little more dramatically.

The mullah started the call to prayer: '*Allah o Akbar, Allah o Akbar*' (God is Great). His high, clear, priest's voice rang out like a bugle, a call to God, but also a call to arms. The two ranks of young men dropped to their knees and then bowed to touch their foreheads on the ground in the traditional act of worship which I found extremely moving. I felt it was not only a daily reaffirmation of their simple faith but also a pledge of their determination to continue to the bitter end the fight against the Russians, whatever the cost in suffering to themselves and their families.

Charles scrambled to his feet and moved the camera round behind the group, giving us a wonderful shot into the evening light, the kneeling mujahideen silhouetted against the green curve of the river, with the mountains rising beyond.

I walked back to the village feeling enormously pleased. We had not only started filming but we had achieved, I was sure, a very moving sequence.

Nigel's outburst about the food may have made Yahya feel guilty, at any rate next morning we had the best breakfast of the trip: a big bowl of whey, oil bread and a dish of the most delicious honey I think I have ever eaten. It was dark golden brown and mixed with bits of the comb, giving it a wonderfully rich, chewy taste. Like all our meals, this was a communal feast, and the fastest and strongest eaters came off best, scooping up gobs of honey with chunks of bread and bolting them down.

Immediately after breakfast we filmed Jean-Philippe giving one of his impromptu clinics in the room next door. The first child was very puny and screamed loudly when Jean-Philippe pulled up its shirt and prodded its stomach. After a rapid diagnosis (he seemed to be able to tell what was wrong at a glance) Jean-Philippe announced the child was suffering from malnutrition, brought on by acute diarrhoea. If unchecked, Jean-Philippe said, the diarrhoea would be fatal. The second child was much less seriously ill and Jean-Philippe guessed that the mother had only brought it along because she had heard there was a foreign doctor in the neighbourhood. Mirabuddin, who Jean-Philippe said was almost able to cope on his own, dished out a ration of pills to both mothers and they went off clutching them with that look of deep satisfaction that a visit to the doctor seems to generate even among more sophisticated patients.

Jean-Philippe spoke English with a heavy French accent but we managed quite a telling interview in which he declared that many Afghans suffered from nervous headaches, brought on by the bombing. The children in particular were prone to symptoms of trauma and he described treating one child, wounded in the arm by bomb splinters, who had not been able to utter a sound. But, he said, the surprising thing was that, despite these psychological effects, the morale of the people, even the refugees, remained extremely high. 'They are poor people, but they are *for* the mujahideen,' he insisted.

I was anxious to get down to the main valley as quickly as possible to see if the Russians had really withdrawn, so we set off at a good pace. It was as usual, a magnificent day, the river sparkling green and silver below us, but the landscape was strangely empty, the villages deserted as if struck by the plague. I realized the people had all fled before the Russian advance and that explained the almost breathless hush, the hint of menace in that tranquil landscape. Near the *qarârgâh*, where we had cooked our soup and which was now a total ruin, we were shown an unexploded bomb. It had been discovered by some boys from the nearby village and was a huge evil-looking lump of metal that seemed to be almost unmarked by its crash landing among the boulders of a dry river bed. I guessed it to be a thousand-pounder – half a ton of high explosive. The mujahideen would open it up, extract the high explosive and use it to increase the power of their Chinese mines.

Reaching the confluence of the Darra and Hazara, we saw that the Russian tanks had indeed got this far: their tracks were plainly visible in the shingle of the river bed. It was hard to say how many there had been, but I guessed a squadron or two – say ten or fifteen, plus armoured personnel carriers. The brothers' village of Tambonnah looked as if a hurricane had swept it: the houses had been bombed or shelled, and some had also been burned. But it was the blast that had wreaked most havoc, smashing down whole trees like twigs. It must have been a terrifying experience to have been caught in that gale of steel.

At Do Ab, where the Darra joins the Panjsher, we crossed the big bridge (presumably the Russians had not destroyed it because they found it useful for their tanks) and said goodbye to Mirabuddin. He was going home to his family at Astana, not knowing whether he would find his home still standing and his parents alive or dead. He was a remarkable young man, his rather colourless manner concealing an intelligent mind and considerable determination. He had helped us far above the call of duty, in the long search for our camera, and I had promised him my Sony short-wave radio as a present when we left. His eyes had brightened in anticipation. The only other person to have such a radio in the Panjsher was Masud himself.

We stopped briefly to rest at the village of Omarz above the bridge, just as a big flock of sheep, many of them fat-tailed, came past in a cloud of dust. They were rather elegant, with delicate heads, necks and slender legs, and their large heavy, swaying tails seemed an incongruous appendage. Most of the houses in Omarz had been gutted by the passing Russian and Afghan column, some had been set on fire and the contents scattered about – bedding, clothes, dishes, the pitifully simple possessions of a peasant community. The word from other wayfarers was that the Russians had withdrawn to

Rokha, the main town at the entrance to the valley, which they had captured in the early summer offensive and from where they had launched the current attack. We also heard that Masud was at the village of Shawa a few miles further up, so we dragged ourselves wearily to our feet and trudged off up the road.

It was at Shawa that the mujahideen had ambushed the Russians in the first offensive and the half-dozen shattered A.P.C.s and the crippled T62 tank still testified to their famous victory. The Russians had not bothered to recover them, perhaps not wanting to expose themselves to the possibility of another ambush. Mujahideen headquarters were higher up, so we left the road and started to climb up the side valley. Stéphane, whom I had persuaded to act as our interpreter for the rest of the trip, for a fee of one thousand dollars, now recounted that the mujahideen at Shawa had suffered a heavy defeat and that Masud had come to get a first-hand account of what had gone wrong. Apparently, the Russians had outflanked a party of about twenty mujahideen on the mountain above us, taken them by surprise when they were all resting, and killed them all, including one of Masud's ablest commanders.

We toiled up the narrow path, the mountain rising steeply on our right, a narrow stream brawling among the rocks on our left. It reminded me very forcibly of Scotland, the cascading, crystal-clear torrent, the granite rocks, the trees overhanging the water's edge, the sudden darting flight of a bird like a dipper. In the late afternoon, with the setting sun still bright in the narrow valley, we crossed the river and climbed a short, steep stretch to a house perched on the side of the hill, surrounded by trees and a few tiny, stony fields. There was an air of bustle; a group of mujahideen came out to shake hands, and I walked forward expecting to catch sight of Masud.

'He's gone', Tom informed me before I could put the question. 'Left two hours ago.'

I sank down on the proffered seat.

'Damn, just our luck. Where's he gone?'

'Oh, over the mountain to another village. It's five hours' walk away – that's for him. He'll be half-way there by now. We'd never catch him.'

I accepted the glass of tea someone had pushed in my hand, and took stock of the situation.

'We can stay the night here,' Yahya said, pointing to an army tent in the field just below us. It was almost hidden by two or three big walnut trees, their dark green foliage providing perfect camouflage.

'Tomorrow,' I said, 'we can film the tank and the A.P.C.s by the bridge and the village that we passed through, the one with the façade of houses that looked completely gutted.'

'Omarz,' Yahya volunteered. 'I will send a message to Masud telling him that we are here and asking what we should do next.'

After tea, we carried our belongings to the big tent and spread our sleeping bags on the sandy earth of the field. Various Afghans arrived to share the tent and our dinner of rice and goat, but morale was so much better now we had our equipment and had started shooting, that we did not mind about the inconvenience as much as we would have done before. The making of the documentary and our return journey were uppermost in our minds.

After dinner, Yahya introduced me to a young lawyer from Herat, who was part of a mujahideen group that had been operating near the Salang Tunnel. The tunnel had fascinated me since I had become interested in Afghanistan and I had originally planned to film there. It was now clear that we simply did not have time: it would take three or four days to get there, another three or four days waiting for some action, if we were lucky, and the same time to get back. The Salang Tunnel was a vitally important supply route and knowing this, the Russians guarded it well, patrolling the area with helicopter gunships. It was high up, around eleven thousand feet, ran for nearly two miles through a western spur of the Hindu Kush and was a vital part of the strategic road system, also built by the Russians in the sixties and seventies. The mujahideen harried the approaches to the tunnel, ambushing Afghan lorries carrying food and goods to Kabul; but they tended to avoid Russian convoys – they were too heavily protected.

Around 6.30 next morning, while we were waiting for breakfast, we were intrigued to see that next to the tent was an open-air workshop, with the barrels of several Russian machine guns scattered about. There was a very large Zigoyak, several Dashakas and a light machine gun (a PK) which the Afghans called a Pika. As we inspected this arsenal, a man came down the steps from the house, sat down cross-legged and started to carve a piece of walnut with a hammer and chisel. It was soon obvious that he was cutting out a stock for a rusty-looking Pika that the mujahideen had unscrewed from an armoured car.

'There's a ready-made sequence for you,' Nigel said. I agreed and within minutes Charles and Tom were shooting.

The Afghan, whose name was Aziz Mohammed, worked fast. Within half an hour he had whittled the block of walnut down to the exact shape and fitted it to the machine gun. It was a neat job executed with only a few tools. Aziz Mohammed's story backed up the claim that Masud's reputation far transcended the confines of the Panjsher Valley. He had owned a little shop making and repairing scissors in Kabul and one day, decided to visit the Panjsher Valley to learn at first hand about this man called Masud. While he was with the mujahideen, a guerrilla brought him a broken Kalakov rifle, the latest Russian model. He not only repaired it but did it so well that Masud, impressed, had asked him to stay in the Panjsher and work for him as a gunsmith. Masud, he said, had promised him a full set of tools, but, he grinned, they had not come yet. With them he would be able to do much more.

It was encouraging to have another, albeit short, sequence 'in the can' and we set off down the valley in high spirits. We made good time to the bridge and spent an hour filming, while our mujahideen escort amused themselves by clambering over the abandoned Russian tank and sitting on the long barrel of its gun like children. They were like children in another way too, becoming temperamental when asked to help carry our equipment. In theory, it had all been arranged before we left the *qarârgâh*. Three of them would carry the camera, the recorder and the tripod. But when we had finished by the bridge and announced that we wanted to walk on to Omarz, one mujahid promptly vanished and the other two made it plain that they did not see themselves in the role of porters. Their manner clearly implied that if we wanted to film Omarz we would have to carry the equipment ourselves. I lost my temper and raged at their disobedience.

'If they don't want to carry the bloody stuff, why the hell did they come with us in the first place?' Finally, we each picked up a piece of equipment and set off down the road, the mujahideen following sheepishly behind.

Omarz lay in a little grove of mulberry trees, a hundred yards from the river, and as we approached along the dusty road, the village seemed to be almost completely deserted. Then I caught sight of a couple of men sitting outside a shop. The wooden door was locked but a line of steel hooks, all empty except for one from which hung a small lump of reddish goat meat, revealed that it was a butcher's. Although half a dozen large, black and yellow striped hornets were

feasting on the meat, the pangs of hunger were so great that I toyed
with the idea of buying it for our dinner.

We moved a few yards further on to get a shot of the line of ruined
houses above the road. They made me think of film-set houses: there
was something unreal about them, as if they were only one-
dimensional, a façade. All we could hear was the sound of the wind.

At the other end of the village, the houses and shops near the road
had been smashed open or gutted with fire, the charred beams lying
amid piles of earth and stones. We climbed up on to a flat roof and
looked down on more scenes of destruction. As Charles was getting
ready to film, there was shouting from the street below and a cloud of
pink smoke rose in the air; someone had let off a Russian smoke flare
and the excitement recreated for an instant the feeling that the
village was still under attack. We could hear the Afghans shouting
and even laughing. Their resilience in the face of adversity never
failed to amaze me.

One of the mujahideen now announced to Stéphane that Yahya
had arranged for us to have lunch further up the valley.

'Not at Shawa?' I asked.

'No,' Stéphane replied, 'they are short of food here. But we can eat
at another house, an hour's walk from here.'

'An hour from here?' I gasped. There was a chorus of dismay from
the others. We debated earnestly.

'Is it a real hour, or an Afghan hour?' someone asked.

'We may walk for two hours and find the food's no good when we
get there,' Nigel said. Stéphane assured us that special arrangements
had been made and the food would probably be good, so hunger
finally overcame weariness. We dumped our equipment with a
friendly young man, in what seemed to be the only undamaged house
in Shawa, watched him lock the door on the precious camera, and set
off up the road.

A few hundred yards ahead, the sound of a muezzin's call to
prayer floated across the midday stillness. This was something I had
always wanted to film, ever since I had started working in television.
The magic of this moment, when the muezzin lifts up his voice to call
the faithful to prayer, had intrigued me ever since I had read E.M.
Forster's marvellously evocative description in *A Passage to India*. But
every time I had tried I had been foiled by the hideous modern habit
of blaring the call from the top of the minaret by loudspeaker. It may
save the muezzin a long climb and his electronically amplified voice

may carry much further, but for me at any rate, it turned a moment of poetry into something mechanical and vulgar. Here in Afghanistan, where they had none of these new-fangled devices, I realized I might satisfy my long-cherished ambition. As we approached I listened carefully. The mullah's voice was excellent – rich, clear and sonorous. We stopped outside the humble roadside mosque, and I asked whether it would be possible to film him when we came back. The mullah beamed. Of course. He would be delighted to let us film him making his evening call at four. His only reservation was that we should not film inside the mosque because the Russians had looted it and left it in disarray. We agreed, shook hands with great warmth and marched determinedly on.

After three-quarters of an hour we found ourselves in a village shaded by enormous mulberry trees. I remembered it from our first drive up the valley in Masud's jeep. It turned out that our mujahid escort did not know exactly where the lunch-house was, only that it was somewhere on the other side of the river: he pointed to a village on the hillside about half a mile away. We sat down under the trees while he went off to investigate.

After a short time he reappeared on the far side of the river, and shouted for us to cross. We walked upstream to the bridge: it was a typical Afghan bridge, with two very long tree trunks cantilevered across the fast-flowing river and anchored in stone piers at either end. The plank was about twelve to fifteen inches wide at the start, but by the time I reached the middle it had narrowed to around nine inches. I have a good head for heights and a good sense of balance, but I began to hesitate. By the time I was three-quarters of the way over, the bridge had narrowed to six inches and I was beginning to wobble. Although I deliberately did not look at the river, I was conscious of it as a fast-moving blur far below and that somehow disorientated me. I covered the last few yards by side-stepping, before making a grateful leap on to solid ground.

I looked back to see Nigel stuck half-way across. He had also turned sideways but was transfixed, gazing down at the water and trembling uncontrollably. I remembered that he suffered from vertigo and realized he must be undergoing agonies. I moved to the end of the bridge and tried to urge him on, but he did not reply, and remained frozen where he was. I measured the drop with my eye. About twenty feet. The river was not very deep, perhaps four feet, and liberally strewn with large boulders, but I thought if he could avoid those, the speed of the water would prevent him hurting himself, although it might whirl him for thirty or forty yards downstream. Then, just when I thought he must fall, he suddenly moved, and side-stepped his way to safety.

After that, lunch might have been an anti-climax, but Yahya had done his work well. We were received by a courtly old Afghan in a white robe and beard to match, whose grandson, aged seven or eight, entertained us until the food arrived. When it came it was copious and delicious: soup, boiled mutton, tomato and onion salad and *mast*. We ate and ate – gorged would be more accurate – until we fell back against our pillows. I had eaten so much that my stomach was actually sore. Then, just when I was contemplating another cup of sweet tea and perhaps a brief snooze, a man appeared with an urgent message from Yahya. It said 'Come as quickly as possible to Sangana [about four hours' march away]. I have the rest of your things. Masud wants you to go to Rokha.'

11

Although we were in a hurry to start, our host insisted on showing us some of the effects of the recent bombing. Huge craters pitted the ground, and the blast had uprooted large trees and hurled debris over a wide area. Several houses had been hit and reduced to piles of rubble and half a dozen villagers had been killed. The only thing that had prevented higher casualties and greater destruction was the layout of the village – the houses were clustered together in groups of four or five with large open spaces between, so that the target area was both large and diffuse.

On our way back (we crossed much lower down and by a much wider bridge) we passed the wreckage of a Russian jet fighter – a MIG 21 – which had come down in the first offensive. The Afghan pilot had baled out and been captured. It was the only downed plane we saw, although the mujahideen claimed many more.

We walked for the first hour or so beside the river, in the shade of giant mulberry and walnut trees, at one point passing a man fishing from the bank. He was the only person I saw fishing during our entire stay but, as Jean José never tired of explaining, there are no trout south of the Hindu Kush and, indeed, although I often examined the rivers in the Panjsher, which looked ideal for trout or even salmon, I never saw a single fish.

We crossed near Shawa on a bridge that by Afghan standards was wide and solid, discovered that Yahya had collected our equipment and marched on in the failing light towards Sangana. Ahead, to the west, the mountains stood out clearly against the pale lemon sky and, as we rounded the bend at Do Ab, where the river makes a wide sweep, the 'V' of the valley opened before us like the entrance to a new world.

We arrived at Sangana in the half dark but, remembering it from our first night in the valley, found its secret paths less mysterious. We were led upstairs to a big room which was full of bearded men wearing turbans and gowns, who all rose to shake hands. I found myself next to Yahya, wedged in between a group of Commanders from the north, from Kunduz and Hannabad, who had brought Masud their moral support and, more important, money.

Tom, on the other side of the room, sat next to a local Commander who produced two letters taken from the body of a young Russian soldier. Tom, who had studied Russian at school, although he claimed to have forgotten most of it, thought the writer was complaining about the hardships of a soldier's life in Afghanistan. The exact translation had to wait until we got back to London. It turned out to be a fascinating and uncensored account of the war as seen through the eyes of a twenty-year-old Russian conscript; it was uncensored presumably because it had never been posted.

Greetings from the Democratic Republic of Afghanistan!

Hello Shura,

Greetings from your soldier friend Yuri: Shura, you promised to write but you forgot, you lazy sod: I suppose you've been living it up where you are, while here we're up to our necks in muck and bullets. We've arrived in a new place, not far from Almaznaya. The worst thing is that they aren't Dushman [bandits] round here, they are mercenaries. They've got DSKs [heavy machine guns] and mortars, and sometimes they have us so tightly pinned down that we feel well and truly buggered. Four of our lads have been killed and our commissar, Batueev, was blown up by a mine. There was almost nothing left of him afterwards. As for your battalion – it's being slowly hammered into the ground.

I won't write much, it's impossible to describe everything. . . How's civvy life going? Did you get your teeth replaced? Dinka and Grinya send you greetings but are offended of course: everyone promised, but no one has written so far. Everything's just bloody fine here and we're counting the days till demob'. Then it'll be home for all, won't it? The three of us will drop in on you, okay? Shura, could I borrow your parade uniform when we come? We don't have any, we've got nothing. We'll only be given battle dress, so where will we find the badges and other stuff?

Shura, do write to me, dare I hope or not? Will you? If there's any problem, I can send you my address again. Please Shura, write to the three of us at least once a month. Is it too much to ask? That's it for now. By the way, the third company has been wiped out. They're all either lying in hospital or in tin boxes. Goodbye, we embrace you strongly,

Yuri, Dima, Grigory.

15.7.82.

Before retiring to bed, Yahya introduced a smiling gentleman called Ali. He was an experienced guide, spoke good English and had walked all over the north the previous summer with a French 'journalist'.

'Six months,' Ali said, with his innocent smile. 'It was a very long walk.' Some journalist, I thought; more likely a French intelligence agent. Mr Ali, as he almost immediately became known, had worked in the Intercontinental Hotel in Kabul as a floor supervisor. Perhaps it was this training that gave him his slightly unctuous manner.

I woke to the sound of goats bleating just below our window. I knew they brought the animals in overnight because, as I had groped my way across the courtyard during the night, I had almost tripped over the family cow. It was difficult to get one's bearings in the dark and to know exactly where to go to answer the call of nature. We discovered later that the correct area was on the outskirts of the village and I suppose we were unpopular because, out of ignorance, we would sometimes leave our mark in the wrong place. Occasionally our hosts would show us the correct spot, although usually they would merely point in the general direction, but often we would be caught short by forces beyond our control and in those cases it was the first tree to hand.

After breakfast and shortly before eight, we set off in the direction of Rokha at the bottom of the valley, our camera and other equipment loaded on two donkeys. I felt a thrill of pleasure, all my senses intensely alive, as we walked in the wonderfully limpid morning light, the mountains so bare and stark and the Panjsher River, green and flashing, fast-running and clear. A mile or so from Sangana we came to the village of Astana, its houses scattered among the trees on the lower slopes of the mountain.

We rested under some trees, munching apples, and then hiked on round a great expanse of sand and shingle in which the river was almost lost to sight. Beyond the bend lay Bazarak, the second village of the valley. It looked as if an earthquake and hurricane had hit it simultaneously: most of the houses were in ruins and the bridge had been destroyed, although the Russians had thrown a pontoon over the gap. A Russian tank lay in the river fifty feet below, where it had been blown by a mine, its turret and gun, which had been ripped off by the force of the explosion, lying beside it. On the far side of the bridge, the school looked as if it had sustained several direct hits at point-blank range and in the courtyard another tank had been blasted by a mine, its gun barrel also torn off.

Mr Ali was jumpy about us staying too long so, after a brief rest, we started to climb up a narrow side valley which had also felt the full weight of the Russian Blitz.

In the afternoon we eventually came to a small group of houses clinging to the rock. They looked remote enough to be immune from the war, but there was a big crater in a field just before the village. We climbed up between the rocks, crossed a slender drawbridge and ducked through a narrow doorway into a room overlooking the river. It was carpeted and strewn with large bright-coloured cushions but there were also gaping holes in the walls and ceiling – the result of a Russian air strike.

Our host was a friendly, cheerful man who said he had worked as a cook for a Western embassy in Kabul. Our thoughts inevitably and immediately turned to food and when dinner arrived, our hopes were more than realized – mutton, soup, potatoes and rice. But our host, who spoke a little English, was very sensitive about his womenfolk. Or perhaps his women were the sensitive ones. At any rate, we were asked not to leave our room without alerting him, as otherwise we might surprise the women and catch them unveiled. Despite the hospitality, we always felt prisoners, never quite acceptable to our Afghan hosts. Stéphane, with his excellent Farsi and knowledge of things Afghan, was the exception.

I do not know if I had eaten too fast, or if the meat was off, but I woke during the night with acute stomachache, necessitating a journey to the outside privy. To complicate matters, a terrific storm broke. At first, as the thunder rolled and the lightning flashed, I thought the Russians had launched a full-scale attack. Then the rain started to hiss down, and by the time I returned from my visit to the privy, it was dripping steadily through the shattered roof. Nigel, who was sleeping in the middle, was cursing as he tried to manoeuvre his sleeping bag into a drier position.

Next morning, Sunday 19 September, our fortieth day in Afghanistan, our smiling host appeared bearing, by popular request, several large plates of chips. Charles crowed with delight and we all gathered hastily round the table cloth, which was spread on the floor. They were excellent potatoes and the chips were fat, oily and very hot. We were glad of their sustenance since we had a long march ahead of us, over a high pass to another valley above Rokha.

After the night's storm, the earth was soaking wet and the raindrops glittered on the grass as we crossed the river and made our way uphill in the sunshine. Higher up the mountain, streaks of hailstones made brilliant white patches against the dark rock. The donkey driver, Mr Ali, and the rest of us climbed and climbed, zigzagging up the grassy flank of the mountain. At around thirteen thousand feet we came on a small grass plateau and the primitive stone hut of a herdsman: as in the Alps, they bring the cattle to the high meadows in the early summer, when the snow melts and the new grass pushes through, and stay up until the first snow forces them down to the valleys again for the winter. The herdsman and his family brought us tea and *mast*, Charles's favourite food. He used to give an ecstatic cry of '*mast, mast*' – half order, half prayer, whenever we arrived at a likely spot.

The herdsman's little family had been joined by a small group of refugees, who peered up anxiously when a jet fighter roared over high above us. I was more interested in the silent flight of a family of handsome lammergeier vultures. They wheeled above us effortlessly as we toiled up towards the distant pass, their cruel beaks, yellowish breasts and huge wings with upcurling tips, making them exotic and rather fearsome companions. I imagined, as they planed close over our heads, that they were regarding us with a speculative eye, as a potential meal.

We reached the top of the pass, around fifteen thousand feet, in a flurry of snow and hurried down to the shelter of some rocks, from which we could admire the stupendous view. Charles produced a slab of Kendal Mint Cake which restored our energies and morale. We were by now undoubtedly acclimatized to high altitude (fifteen thousand feet is reckoned to be the height at which altitude sickness usually starts) but perhaps because of my disturbed night, I felt annoyingly weak. Nevertheless we descended at a good pace, and finally reached the *qarârgâh* in the early evening.

Rather surprisingly, the house (for that was all it was) was perched on the side of the mountain in an extremely open and, I would have thought, vulnerable position. The mujahideen crowded round us, a lively and friendly lot, and we shook hands with the commander, a tall man of about thirty. He introduced a wild-looking young man called Gulai Dar who, he said, would take us down the valley the next day to where we could film the Russian positions. Gulai Dar, with his bushy beard and flashing eyes, grinned at the prospect. A little later Charles had a conversation with him and returned full of foreboding.

'This bloke, Gulai Dar, I think he's crazy,' he said. 'I don't think we want to get mixed up with him tomorrow.'

Before we could discuss it further, a shell exploded on the ridge about a mile away.

'Russ. Shurawi. Bombard,' the mujahideen shrugged, displaying all the insouciance of men who have been under fire before.

'Quick,' I said. 'Get the camera.' We set it up outside the *qarârgâh* just in time to film two or three more shells landing and record the ensuing bangs: there was an interval of at least a couple of seconds between the burst and the sound of the explosion.

Next morning, we were up early to find Gulai Dar eager to go. The path led down steeply for a mile or so and then we branched left, climbing to a group of damaged and deserted houses. Gulai Dar urged us on until we came to a shallow grave in a grove of mulberry trees. Pointing and grinning, he gave instructions for the top-soil to be removed to reveal the fully clothed body of a Russian soldier he had killed, the face bloated by decomposition, one hand crooked grotesquely by *rigor mortis*, the eyes protruding in a ghastly stare. The stench was appalling and Gulai Dar stood with his handkerchief clapped over his mouth. Charles filmed under protest.

'We're not going to use this, I hope,' he said. 'This man [Gulai Dar] is a bloody killer and I think it's totally wrong to show it. Particularly since they've dug the body up for us specially.'

In some respects I had to agree, but I still thought it would be right to show the dead Russian. After all, this was a savage war on both sides and if we were to refuse to show its grim and possibly disgusting face, we would be failing in our duty to report the facts.

In the heat and strain our tempers flared and I found myself saying: 'After all, nobody asked the bloody Russians to come here. They've invaded Afghanistan. They're the occupiers and the Afghans have every right to kill them.' Unaware of our argument, Gulai Dar led us on down the hill, pushing through the dense undergrowth.

'Where the hell are we going?' someone asked. I had to confess I did not know myself.

'Tank?' I snapped at Gulai Dar as he scrambled ahead of me like a goat. 'Russ tank?' and I made as if to hold a camera.

He nodded emphatically and pointed.

'Not far,' someone translated, 'and you will see several Russian tanks. You can take pictures.' Since that was what we had come for, we were forced to trust our guide and continue on our way.

After a brief stop, Gulai Dar and his mujahideen picked up their weapons and set off again. We emerged on the bare hillside and followed an irrigation channel across the side of the mountain, bending low where the cover was thin, conscious of being overlooked by the steep mountains that ring Rokha. On some, we were told, the Russians had lookout posts.

We came to a narrow gully that plunged between the rocks and Gulai Dar left half his men in the shade of an overhang, beckoning us to follow. Carrying camera, recorder and tripod, we slithered down the dried-up bed of the stream, traversed some scree and ended on a bare crag that jutted out over the valley. Gulai Dar crawled to the outer edge and waved to us to follow. I crept forwards and peered over the edge. About half a mile away, parked in a line facing us, were several Russian tanks, their guns pointing in our direction. I guessed they formed the outer defences of Rokha. Gulai Dar scanned the hill-top opposite, searching for enemy activity. Charles wrestled the camera up the rock and tried to find a comfortable position from which to film. I trained the binoculars on the tanks and described the scene to Charles, as he struggled to line up the camera and focus.

'Four tanks in a row,' I recited. 'There's a soldier walking right across in the open behind the middle tank now. . . .'

'Shhh,' Charles ordered. 'I'm running.'

With only the brush of the wind against the crag to break the silence, we lay still, watching the unsuspecting Russians.

Charles stopped filming and I continued my commentary.

'There's a roadblock by the tank on the left and then, about a hundred yards behind, you can see a house, looks like a C.P. [Command Post] and a lorry or A.P.C. in the shade. Quite a few troops on it, as far as I can make out.'

'Okay, I'm going to do some close-ups,' Charles announced and we all fell silent again. Tom was concentrating hard, trying to record the silence of the mountain without getting the boom that wind invariably produces on a microphone. Nigel was busy taking stills. When we had all we needed, we backed carefully off the rock and toiled sweating up the steep gully. Gulai Dar, who had left three men on the crag below, led us to a terrace planted with young peach trees, from which we had a commanding view of the crag.

Still grinning, Gulai Dar gestured that this was the best place to set up the camera. He raised his hands, 'Pam, pam,' to show that the mujahideen below would, at a given signal, open fire on the Russians.

When we were ready the mujahideen opened up, their PK light machine gun and AK47s sounding like peashooters. Puffs of smoke drifted off the crag. After a few moments, the men with the AKs crawled back a few yards to reload, then edged forward and opened up again.

'Pap-pap-pap-pap-pap-pap. . . .' The sound bounced off the rocks around us. Charles was as tight on the zoom lens as we could go. I felt unheroically nervous, wondering when the Russians would start shooting back, and to allay my fear, I greedily ate peach after peach, the juice dribbling down my chin on to my shirt. Finally, when Charles said he had enough film, Gulai Dar seized the tripod and led us back along the terrace to the path and steeply upwards to the big overhang. As we climbed panting, the first salvo of Russian mortars or tank rounds slammed into the hillside above us. Charles wanted to stop to film but Gulai Dar hurried us upwards, determined to get to the best and safest vantage point.

I could not help being impressed by the way in which, although he had probably never seen television, he immediately understood what we needed to make a film. Having arrived at the overhang, he put down the tripod and, grinning broadly, enthusiastically indicated where the return fire would fall. Sure enough it did, grenades and mortars making sharp cracks as they burst on the rocky hillside, the wind immediately sweeping away the smoke. It was extremely difficult to anticipate precisely where the rounds would land, even with me acting as spotter, and in a way the sound track of the battle was more impressive. At one point, to generate a little more excitement, Gulai Dar leaped a ditch, sprinted up the hillside and blazed away with his Kalakov. I noticed that his boot was split open to reveal a thickly bandaged toe and he explained afterwards that he had been wounded four times, twice by the viciously tumbling bullet of the Kalakov (the AK74).

The shooting died away and we started the climb back to the

qarârgâh: there was no point in hanging about, the Russians might call in the jets or the helicopter gunships. As we followed the irrigation channel back across the hillside, we filmed a group of Russians or Afghans walking in single file along the skyline of the mountain opposite.

Two hours later we were back in the *qarârgâh*, tired but jubilant after our morning's work. Because of the delay in getting the camera, it was the only action sequence we had on moving picture.

'I feel much, much happier,' Nigel exulted. 'Without that sequence I would doubt very much that we had a programme. With it, I feel confident we have. I think we're over the hump.'

But we had not finished for the day. The irrepressible Gulai Dar wanted to show off his latest toy, a captured Russian automatic grenade launcher, an AGS 17. He set it up in a hollow above the *qarârgâh* and loosed off several rounds. By the end of the afternoon, we were all as impressed by Gulai Dar as we had been apprehensive twenty-four hours before. He obviously was not crazy, but an extremely brave man and a very able commander. Four years before, as an eighteen-year-old, he had worked in a bakery in Kabul. His special job was to crimp the bread – making a pretty pattern of fingermarks – before it was baked in the big earthenware ovens set in the ground. Now he was a seasoned guerrilla fighter and, although only twenty-two, had seen a lot of action. The Rokha area, being the most fought over, undoubtedly held the best of Masud's guerrillas.

In anticipation, we had earlier asked Mr Ali if he could arrange a couple of chickens for dinner. Everything we ate seemed to be boiled – boiled rice, boiled goat, boiled potatoes – so, on this occasion, we asked, as a special favour, if we could have roast chicken. Our mouths watered at the mere thought. Mr Ali entered into long negotiations with the cook, a rather bossy man in whose house we were staying. Two tins of Russian 'grease' (vegetable oil, we supposed) were purchased and elaborate preparations made.

Then Nigel returned from an outdoor visit to announce, 'They're boiling the chickens.'

'But they're supposed to be roasting them,' I contradicted from my seat on the floor.

'I know, Sandy, but I've just had a look and they're boiling them.'

I could not be bothered to get up and have a look, but Charles did a bit later. He returned to report, 'Well, they may have been boiling them before, but they're roasting them now. And doing potatoes.'

Eventually Mr Ali appeared and announced in his best Intercontinental manner: 'Dinner is ready.'

We sat up, tucked our legs out of the way – something I always found extremely difficult – and made room for the cloth to be unfurled. It was always done with something of a flourish, notwithstanding the fact that it was usually rather grubby. The chicken was brought in, together with potatoes and the bread, and we tucked in hungrily.

'It's like rubber,' Nigel said. 'Totally inedible.' I seized a bit of breast and worried it with my teeth.

'Delicious,' I rejoined. 'Very, very good indeed.' Nigel looked at me disbelievingly. I persevered. It was tough, but tasty and I was damned hungry.

After dinner, Stéphane announced in conspiratorial tones that Masud's secretary, who had arrived that afternoon, had told him in confidence that Masud was expected in Parende the next day and there was every chance we would see him. My spirits soared. If we could get Masud on film, we would be well on the way to having a first-class documentary.

Encouraged by our tiresomely bossy host, we were up very early, and left without breakfast, Mr Ali saying we would stop further up. We did, in a sort of stone lean-to. We crept inside to find ourselves on thick, rich-red carpets and were served hot, sweet milk tea and fresh bread. The family were refugees from Rokha, driven out by the fighting.

It was a long haul up to the pass, even the donkeys finding it a struggle, and by the time we got to the top, Tom and Stéphane, who took pleasure in walking faster than the rest of us, had disappeared. This slightly annoyed me as I wanted to get a shot of the magnificent panorama of peaks, their north faces dusted with snow. Charles set up the camera and with me acting as soundman, we shot it on the last power in the batteries. At one point an invisible Russian jet thundered high overhead while a pair of eagles circled silently above us.

Nigel was climbing very slowly and while we waited for him we ate scraps of bread and the delicious cream cheese Mr Ali had bought on the way up. He arrived eventually, had his share of cheese and took pictures. Then we set off on the very steep descent, past small drifts of hailstones, heading for the meadows far below. The lammergeiers reappeared, winging their stately way above us, waiting, we felt, for one of us to make a fatal slip.

We came to the herdsman's shelter in the early afternoon, to find Tom and Stéphane stretched out on the grass, having lunched off fresh butter and milk tea. We passed round our cheese and more tea was produced. Nigel got Mr Ali to take a picture of us all and it came out like a holiday snap. We are lying there, in the sunshine, looking disgustingly healthy, with no sign of hardship or suffering on our faces. On the final descent to Parende, we again lost Tom and Stéphane, arriving in the early evening to be greeted by our English-speaking host like long-lost friends.

Tom and Stéphane had made a detour to find Masud, who was staying at a house about half an hour's walk away, and reappeared to announce that he would be coming to our house for supper. He arrived after dark, his bodyguard with him. It was the first time we had seen him since our meeting in the cave, early in the Russian advance. He came into the room radiating his usual energy, shook hands with everybody and sat down: dinner was promptly served. As always when Masud appeared, the host had made a special effort, killing if not the fatted calf, at least some sort of sheep. We ate well.

After the meal, over tea, Masud talked a lot and seemed in good spirits. I asked him why he thought the Russians had withdrawn so soon and he said, for two reasons. First, they had believed that the mujahideen were in disarray after the first offensive, both in terms of weapons and morale. Second, the Russians firmly believed that once they appeared on the scene, the Panjsheri would forsake the mujahideen and flock to the side of the Government. When they discovered that both suppositions were completely wrong and that the mujahideen were still determined to fight, they had withdrawn. What about casualties? Masud said that the Russians had suffered heavy losses, but he had no figures yet: rather than guess, he preferred to wait until he got the official figures from his sources in Kabul. . . . It was clearly one of his great strengths, and one of the Russians' most serious weaknesses, that the Afghan Army and Ministry of Defence were riddled with mujahideen agents and sympathizers. It was another bitter parallel with Vietnam, since there, nothing the Americans told their South Vietnamese allies was secret. Here, anything the Russians told their Afghan allies was immediately leaked to the Resistance. It seemed to me to give Masud, and the mujahideen generally, a huge advantage.

12

Masud had agreed to be interviewed the following day and we were up early in preparation. He arrived at eight but went straight into conference with the local mujahideen in the next-door room. Charles and I walked up the hill to find a suitable interview spot, and chose one beside a bombed-out house, with a view of the mountains behind.

'The earlier we can do it the better, because of the light,' Charles reminded me.

I hovered anxiously outside the conference room but the discussions dragged on interminably and it was not until ten that Masud reappeared.

I immediately buttonholed him and said in French, 'Can we do the interview now? Before the sun is too high.'

'*Oui, oui,*' he said. '*Je viens toute de suite.*'

But it took another ten minutes to get him up the hill and the light was already becoming hard. Everyone we passed wanted to talk and he always listened. It struck me that Masud might be a guerrilla leader by force of circumstances, but essentially he was a politician. I was sure he agreed with Clausewitz that war was an extension of politics.

The interview posed various technical problems. I had decided it would have to be done in Farsi so that Masud could express himself as freely as possible. I would put the question in English, Stéphane would translate into Farsi, Masud would reply and Stéphane would give me a brief résumé in English – no more than a couple of sentences. In this way I would get a rough idea of what Masud was saying, although probably not enough to ask an intelligent supplementary. When we got back to London I would have Masud's answers translated verbatim into English and choose the bits I wanted. Finally, when it had all been edited, the audience would see Masud on the screen, but hear his words spoken in English by a disembodied voice. This sounds complicated, but it was the only way to achieve the desired results.

I started off by asking Masud about the importance of Islam to the Resistance. Islam was vital, he replied. It was the foundation and the driving force. Masud made two other fundamental points. One was that eighty per cent of his weapons were captured, or bought, from the Russians. The other was that the mujahideen badly needed portable ground to air missiles, like the British Blowpipe, to counter Soviet aircraft and particularly helicopters. (This, of course, could revolutionize the war, but it seems that neither the West nor General Zia in Pakistan want to raise the ante in this way.)

I was impressed by how natural Masud was in front of the camera. He wanted to know only the broad outline of the questions and then took them as they came, answering freely and with great conviction. He also looked the part of the dashing young guerrilla leader.

When we had finished, Abdul Sattar, a young mine expert, set off a Russian trip-flare which howled like a Banshee and shot incandescent star shells into the blue sky. Masud laughed and then walked down the hill to the house, stopping to greet and talk to people on the way, like a popular politician in his constituency. He was in his element and very much at ease. Inside, we found him crouched in the front room beside a tall, bushy-bearded mujahid, with a white-bandaged stump protruding from one trouser leg. We shook hands, Masud explaining that Abdul Wahid was one of his senior commanders, who had lost his foot while clearing mines in front of a Russian position. He had found two with his probe, lifted one and was just about to lift the other when his foot slipped and set off the mine. Masud told me that he planned to send Abdul Wahid over the mountains to Pakistan, to have a new foot fitted and I chipped in to say that we had a very good hospital near London where they specialized in this sort of thing. It was at Roehampton, for example, that they made and fitted artificial legs for Group Captain Douglas Bader. Masud translated for Abdul Wahid, who immediately straightened up and examined me with new interest.

'I'll look into it as soon as we return,' I told Masud.

Nigel looked at me pointedly.

'That's a commitment if ever I heard one,' he said with satisfaction.

I made light of it. 'I'll call Roehampton when we get back,' I assured the room.

When I got back to England, I did make enquiries, but Abdul Wahid arrived in Peshawar two months later, before I had made any firm arrangements. Then, completely fortuitously, This Is Your Life *decided to mark the publication of my memoirs,* Don't Worry About The Money Now, *by doing a programme on me. At the end of the half-hour show, Eamonn Andrews, clutching his big red book, announced, 'And when you were in Afghanistan last year, making a documentary on the Afghan Resistance, you promised a young guerrilla commander who'd had his foot blown off by a mine, that you would arrange for him to get an artificial foot in Britain. And here he is, he's come all the way from Afghanistan, Abdul Wahid. . . .'*

To my immense surprise Abdul Wahid walked through the studio door on his wooden peg leg and rather self-consciously gave me the double Afghan embrace. High drama. Much applause from the studio audience.

While they were researching the programme, my wife Eleanor had given them all the details and encouraged them to include Abdul Wahid; they eventually tracked him down in Oslo, where he was attending a conference. His new foot, by the way, cost £750 which we raised partly by public subscription.

Masud rose to go, explaining that he had not been feeling well for a couple of days, but that we would leave together for Sangana the following day. At 3.30 the wind rose, the sun dropped behind the mountains and it turned quite cold. As so often happens in Greece about this time of year, the weather was suddenly breaking. The storm of the other night, which had left the first coating of snow on the high peaks, had quite definitely signalled the approach of autumn.

Masud appeared late next morning, just before lunch. His brother Yahya explained that he had a touch of fever and was tired after the recent fighting. He went straight into the room next door, full of mujahideen and other locals. I did not like to disturb him but we needed more shots, so we trailed him up the hillside to another house where he was having lunch with a small group of aides and a local with whom he had a long *sotto-voce* conversation.

Living so publicly, Afghans are adept at having whispered,

apparently private conversations, even in a crowded room, and Masud was especially skilled at this – no doubt because it was essential to his security. That morning, for example, we saw a ten-year-old boy who, the mujahideen said, was a Russian spy. His father worked for the Government in Kabul, and was a good party member. The boy claimed to have been recruited, with three hundred others from all over Afghanistan, and sent to Tashkent, in Uzbekistan near the Afghan border, for training in espionage and sabotage. After the three-month course, he was sent back to Kabul and told to infiltrate himself into the Panjsher Valley. His mission was to collect information on mujahideen positions in the Panjsher and, more important, on Masud's movements. He had arrived in the valley with a story that he was going to visit an aunt who lived in one of the main villages, but a man who befriended him became suspicious when the boy said he could not remember his aunt's name. After further questioning the boy broke down and confessed all. Masud had given instructions that the boy should not be harmed, and planned to send him to the Jamiat school in Pakistan, where he would be given a more traditional Afghan education.

After lunch, as pre-arranged, Masud walked down the hill and, leaping from stone to stone, crossed the river and made ready for prayer. We were waiting for him, with the camera in position, and started filming as soon as he appeared, the long lens lending the scene a sense of secrecy and mystery. Masud took off his scarf and jacket, revealing an automatic in a shoulder holster, and stooped to wash in the cold mountain water. Then he walked towards us, the camera trailing him as he half disappeared behind some bushes, watched him comb his thick hair and check his appearance in a small mirror, and followed him to the little meadow, bright with late summer flowers, where the mujahideen were already assembled.

It was a stunning scene, with the rush of the river in our ears and the sunlit mountains rising starkly like a moonscape against the gentian-blue of the sky. Masud led the prayers, the mujahideen's weapons piled in front of him round the bulbous warhead of an RPG7. It occurred to me that perhaps I had been unfair and the mujahideen did this less for the camera and more as a precaution against surprise attack. After all, a man is rarely more vulnerable than when he is kneeling on the ground, his thoughts on higher things.

After prayers, Masud shook hands with his followers, no doubt giving last-minute instructions to his local commanders, and then bounded back across the river and strode off towards Parende. Tom was indisposed, so I was carrying the recorder and I had to walk flat out to keep up. About a mile downstream we came to a sudden stop. A group of mujahideen were drawn up in a circle under a huge walnut tree and Masud stepped off the path to join them. A long palaver followed, with Masud asking a string of questions and getting rather embarrassed replies from the mujahideen. Finally two very sheepish young men were propelled into the circle and put through the same interrogation process by Masud. He never raised his voice, dominating the proceedings, it seemed to me, by intellect and sheer force of personality.

At the end of the court-martial – for that is what it turned out to be – the two young men, looking even more sheepish, handed over their weapons and filed out of the circle. I asked Yahya what it was all about.

'They were absent from sentry duty last night. They were supposed to be guarding Masud's house,' he told me. 'They have been sentenced to ten days' expulsion from the ranks of the mujahideen.'

Masud got up and led the way downstream. On the two-hour hike to Bazarak, Masud stopped at one point to read a note delivered by a man who came hurrying towards us. They sat on the stones beside the path, Masud perusing the note with great care and then questioning the young, rather shabbily dressed messenger at length. He wrote a reply, handed it to the young man and sent him on his way. Masud then disappeared over a wall to answer the call of nature and I walked on a few hundred yards to wait by a narrow bridge. Suddenly, I heard the sound of gunfire, a staccato, banging sound. The echoes richocheted back from the severe grey mountain above us. I looked back to see Masud trying his hand at a little sharpshooting with a PK. I cursed. The camera was with Charles, who was some way behind, and in any case I had let a burly Afghan from Badakhshan give me a hand with the recorder and he had sprinted so far ahead he was out of sight. I waited for Masud and, all together now, we completed the final stretch to Bazarak, stopping only once to take a shot of him and his men walking purposefully through the bomb-shattered trees just above the village.

Hardly anything in Bazarak had been left standing. As we walked round together, Masud explained that the Russians had dropped leaflets at the start of the second offensive, calling on the local people to come down from the mountains and surrender. Otherwise, the leaflets warned, they would destroy everything. The Russians had certainly done their best to carry out their threat. One house we passed was hardly more than a big pile of rubble. In a field below the village, Masud picked up a handful of wheat grains and displayed them in his palm. They were burnt black; proof, if any were needed, that the Russians were applying a scorched earth policy to the Panjsher.

Next we inspected a Russian tank that lay like a stuck pig in the middle of the school courtyard. Round it the school buildings had been gutted, but whether by shellfire or bombing was impossible to tell. I asked Masud if the tank had been knocked out in the first offensive.

'No, no,' he said. 'Just the other day, in the recent offensive. The mujahideen noticed that the Russian tanks always used to shell their positions on the mountain from here. So they made a very big mine and one night planted it. Next day the Russian tanks came as usual but stopped a few yards away, up there. They thought they had put it in the wrong place. Then this T72 came along and drove right onto the mine. You see what happened.'

I looked at the T72 in some awe. It must have been a terrific explosion to tear the turret off and hurl it, and the gun, several yards, and the heavy steel of the hull had been perforated like a colander.

As we walked back over the bridge I brought up the subject of the Salang Tunnel. We had had a long talk about it with someone from the Embassy in Islamabad. Could the mujahideen blow it up if they wanted to?

'Of course, we could,' Masud sounded optimistic. 'But it is too early. The time to blow up the Salang Tunnel will be in two or three years' time, or maybe four, when we are all around Kabul, ready to take the city. That will be the time to blow up the Salang Tunnel. You know, we can cut the road and ambush convoys on their way through at any time. We planned to do this early in the summer. There are places where the trees come close to the road for several kilometres and it is easy to get close. But the Russian offensive forced us to change our plans.'

'But have you got the technical capacity to blow it up?' I persisted.

'Of course. That's not the problem,' Masud said. 'It's a question of timing.'

I thought of Mao and his theory of guerrilla war: the capital city was the ultimate objective. Like a ripe plum it would fall to the advancing guerrilla armies when they had 'liberated' the rest of the country. It had happened in China; it had happened in Vietnam. Masud was clearly confident it would happen in Afghanistan too, one day.

The jeep arrived and Masud and some of his aides bundled into it. Yahya promised it would come back for us a bit later, but rather than wait, I decided to walk, and he and I set off together. The valley was peaceful in the evening light, the river murmuring softly in the distance, our feet silent in the dust of the road. After a mile or two, we came to Jangalak, Masud's home village. His family house had been badly damaged and we could just see it through the trees.

We sat by the road in the gathering dusk, close to the river, watching the last magical moments of the sunset. To while away the time, I tried my hand at a verse in the Chinese style:

September Evening
The willows by the Panjsher River tremble in the chill breeze,
The mountains of Rokha are sharp against the pale evening light,
The moon's reflection lies broken in the shallow water,
The mujahideen pray, facing Mecca, as the sun sets.

I wondered if Mao would have approved.

It was getting chilly and when Yahya suggested we went inside, I readily agreed. He led me to a nearby house where, in a crowded upstairs room, Masud was holding court with the men of Jangalak. A place was immediately made for me and Masud offered some apples. 'Try one,' he said. 'They're good. They're from my garden.' I ate a couple. They were very good.

They all rose to go outside to pray and I made my way back to the road again. The jeep arrived soon afterwards and I squeezed in the back. Wedged painfully together, we bumped off towards Sangana, the less fortunate ones, among whom I counted myself, being forced to balance on the sharp metal edge of the cushionless back seat. Tom and Stéphane were in the luggage space at the back, among the equipment, whence cries of pain emerged from time to time.

We stopped at one point to allow a mujahid to clear some rocks from the road.

'Mines,' someone explained, but I was unable to understand exactly what he was doing and was too tired to care. Dinner was very late, at 9.30, when we had almost given up hope and gone to bed. But the rice and mutton were above average and the grapes, from a vineyard behind the house, worth waiting for. I was cold and dog-tired by the time I crawled into my sleeping bag and fell asleep almost immediately.

After breakfast, procured by the indefatigable Mr Ali, and with no other pressing engagement, I quizzed him about the greetings that Afghans exchange when they meet one another on the open road. The exchange usually starts with the traditional '*Salaam Aleikum*' (God be with you). To which the answer is: '*Aleikum salaam*' (And with you). Then, looking at you with concern, the other man will say: '*Monda Nabashi?*' (Aren't you tired?). To which the stock reply is: '*Zinda Bashi!*' (I'm still alive). To which your interlocutor adds: '*Che turastin?* (How are you?). And you say: '*Hubastam*' (I'm fine). It can go on almost indefinitely, accompanied by much handshaking, but that is enough to enable a mere foreigner to keep his end up.

Strolling in the village shortly afterwards, I met Masud. After a brief chat, he said, 'Have you time to discuss something with me privately?'

I was rather taken aback. 'Yes, of course. Now?'

'Not here. Go with this mujahid. He will take you to a house and I'll come later. If we are seen together people will talk.'

The mujahid, who had been our first escort to Khenj, smiled and signed to me to follow. I thought Masud's discretion rather strange, but presumed he had his reasons. We walked through the village, the houses pleasantly shaded by the high canopy of walnut and mulberry trees, and turned in at the house of one of Masud's friends.

A few minutes later Masud arrived with the owner and sat down opposite me. It was the first time I had seen him sit on a chair. A huge trayful of beautiful, round, red grapes was brought in and although Masud ate very sparingly, I had difficulty restraining myself as I waited, excitedly, to hear what he wanted to discuss.

'I want to ask you,' he began, 'how we can get help from the West and if you think that the Afghan Resistance will be able to set up committees, like the P.L.O., in the West?'

I said there were already a couple of committees in France and one in Britain – the Afghanistan Support Committee – which I was sure could be expanded. I saw no reason why similar committees should not be set up in other countries, for example, America. As for help from the West generally, I said Mrs Thatcher, President Reagan and President Mitterand of France supported the Afghan Resistance in the sense that they were all opposed to Soviet expansionism. I recalled Mrs Thatcher's reaction to the Soviet invasion of Afghanistan and Lord Carrington's initiative when he went to Moscow and tried to persuade the Russians to withdraw. Masud nodded, implying he was aware of all that.

'I don't know if the West *is* prepared to give the Afghan Resistance military aid, but, if I were in your place, I would appeal directly. If you want to send a message to Mrs Thatcher, for example, I would be happy to take it for you and see it gets to her. Our film could also be very useful, in putting your case to the outside world and I am sure I can arrange for Mrs Thatcher to see it.'

He made no comment and we then talked about Vietnam. I told Masud I had been there several times, and spoke about the amazing tenacity and courage of the Vietcong and North Vietnamese soldiers. 'At the beginning the Americans thought it wouldn't take them long to win the war against such a small country, with inferior equipment. It came as a great shock to them when they found that, despite all their helicopters and all their bombing, they could not defeat what they considered to be a second-rate enemy.'

Masud listened intently, no doubt drawing his own comparisons. When I described the B52 raids, how the giant bombers flying at forty thousand feet would drop huge quantities of bombs, destroying areas half a mile long by a quarter of a mile wide, Masud's eyes gleamed with concentration. When I told him how the B52 raids, ten or more miles away, rattled my hotel windows in Saigon, he turned excitedly to the others in the room and translated.

He talked about his own position with an almost clinical detachment. He said he received very little aid from the outside and claimed the Pakistanis stole a lot of weapons that were destined for him, substituting old rifles instead. 'If we didn't capture and buy a lot from the Russians, we would be in extremely short supply. As it is, we're short of ammunition; we only have about fifty mortar rounds in the entire valley; we're so short, I can't launch an attack on Rokha, as I'd like to do.'

'You say the Russians sell you arms?' I asked in surprise.

'Oh yes, the Afghans usually give them to us, but the Russians sell us Kalashnikovs – even Kalakovs – for money or for hashish.'

'Do many of the Russian soldiers smoke hashish?'

'All of them.' The parallel with the American GIs in Vietnam was irresistible.

I told him how the Vietnamese Communists had received a steady flow of arms from Russia and China throughout the Vietnam War until in the end, the North Vietnamese were better equipped than the South. He drank in every word.

How did he finance his war?

'The money we receive from the sale of emeralds from Dasht-i-Riwat [at the head of the valley] is vital to our war effort.' They were self-supporting in many ways. 'But, if the West were to help us, we would be able to conduct a much more effective war.'

On refugees, Masud said they posed a very big problem. Assuming the total population in the Panjsher Valley to be about eighty thousand, he estimated forty or fifty thousand were refugees and many had lost their houses and belongings. The winter was going to be very bad. They would need help, in fact, if they had not had help already from Andarab to the north, he doubted if they would have managed.

Then he said something that made me sit forward on the edge of my chair.

'If the Russian attacks go on like this, we'll have to change our tactics and conduct a more mobile war. As long as I am here, the Russians will continue to attack the Panjsher. So next spring, I intend to leave the Panjsher and conduct a mobile war against the big Russian bases in the north and north-east. We will hit them hard in their bases. It will be a long war, but we will keep fighting.'

Later Masud explained that he intended to set up three new mobile groups, each of one hundred and fifty men. Each group would have three platoons of thirty men, armed with Kalashnikovs, Kalakovs, light machine guns (PKs) and RPG7s, a small headquarters unit and a heavy weapons squad of fifty men, armed with mortars, artillery, heavy machine guns and AGS 17 grenade launchers.

'We have a lot of work to do this winter,' he said. He got up and shook hands. Later, I asked him to answer one more question on camera.

'If you had the opportunity to make a direct appeal, through television, to the leaders of the West, what would you say?'

He answered: 'The Russians are not interested in Afghanistan for itself. What they really want is what they have always wanted – a warm water port in the Indian Ocean and control of the West's oil supply in the Gulf. So far the West has stood idly by and done nothing to help the Afghans. All we have had from the West is words, not deeds.'

In that stark landscape, with the mountains rising steeply all around us, I felt his words had a terrible ring of truth.

13

All of us were now impatient to complete shooting and start the long journey back to Pakistan. Tom and Stéphane had set off early to round up the rest of our equipment, including the vital battery charger, and to bring everything back to Sangana. Charles and I used up what little power we had left filming the girls of the village playing hopscotch. I had picked out one enchanting child with huge dark eyes and long black hair, but she was terribly shy and froze whenever she realized the camera was on her. She was called Morbori (Pearl in Farsi), and at seven was the eldest of the village mullah's four children. They had all lived happily in Sangana until a few weeks before, when the Russian jets came diving out of the blue sky and bombed the village. They had all run to the outskirts to hide and, although none of the children was hurt, the mother had been killed by a piece of shrapnel.

Other children in the little group had also lost parents in the war. One especially pretty girl in a turquoise dress had lost her father, killed fighting the Russians. There was hardly a child there whose life had not been brutally affected by the war. And all to advance and consolidate the frontiers of the Russian Empire, to shore up the system that Marx, Lenin and Stalin had bequeathed to the twentieth century. Life had often been brutish and short in these mountains, but to bomb these innocent children in the name of peace and democracy seemed, to me, to be the ultimate obscenity.

Masud appeared before lunch with a projector and a French television film on the Panjsher. He asked if we could show it to him. He had had it for months without being able to see it. Charles said we needed the rest of our equipment first. In fact, we did have the portable generator to power the projector but Charles was determined to strike a hard bargain. Masud left saying he would send someone up the Darra Valley to bring down the rest of our stuff but nothing happened.

We dined off some very tasty chicken and were asleep when Tom and Stéphane finally appeared after midnight. They had the battery charger but reported that other bits of equipment were still scattered over the countryside from the Darra to Shawa. Worse, the porters had threatened to mutiny and they had had enormous difficulty in getting any co-operation at all. They had eaten practically nothing all day but, despite their tribulations, were in remarkably good spirits.

Next morning was taken up with charging batteries. Masud departed early for Bazarak in the jeep, so our planned expedition to film a school had to be postponed until the afternoon when the jeep returned. We drove to the bridge at the bottom of the Darra Valley, from where we had to walk to Tambonnah. It turned out to be a long hike, carrying the camera, recorder, spare cassettes and batteries, all of which became extremely heavy. We arrived in the village at around three to find our old friend Sharia, the wispy ideologue from Marar-i-Sharif, in charge. He had obviously been organizing furiously, in anticipation of our visit. A line of men were clearing the rubble left by the latest Russian attack, passing stones from hand to hand, while a group of boys with banners paraded towards us chanting the Jamiat song. It sounded tuneless and repetitive, and they did not seem to know it very well. Sharia and Abdul Hai, who had also appeared, wanted us to film the mujahideen walking through the village in single file. The first time they marched towards us the leading man strutted past the camera in a bad imitation of the goose step: it looked ludicrous. We said they would have to do it again, this time in two lines. Charles got very excited, waving his arms about and Sharia and Abdul Hai became equally worked up. Abdul Hai made a tremendous effort to explain himself in English, failed and lapsed into hurt silence. In the end, the mujahideen formed one line, which they said was the most natural thing, and stalked past us as if they were going off to battle. At least the second time they looked a little less self-conscious.

We then moved under the trees to film an open-air lesson conducted by Sharia. All the men crowded round to watch, which would have ruined the shot, so they all had to be moved. When the lesson did begin it took the form of question and answer, a sort of catechism in which Sharia would pose the questions and the children answered in unison: why were the Afghans fighting the Russians? (to free their country); why were the Russians doomed to failure? (because Allah was on the side of the mujahideen); why were the mujahideen bound to win? (because they were fighting a holy war, a Jehad). The word Jehad rang out from the lips of the young boys like a clarion call. They finished off with a series of slogans, which they shouted in response to an older boy who stood in front of the class and acted as cheerleader.

'Zindebad mujahideen . . . Long live the mujahideen . . . Long live Islam . . .' they chanted and then in a chorus of howls, like young wolves baying for blood, they cried: 'Death to the Russians. Curses on Lenin. Curses on Brezhnev [he died soon afterwards]. Death to Babrak [Karmal, the Afghan President]. Long live Islam!'

Afterwards an old man with a splendid white beard, dressed in a long blue gown and carrying his prized old Lee Enfield 303, posed for a picture. He claimed, with enormous pride, that he and his sister had killed eight Russians when they had attacked their village, picking them off from the hillside. It seemed an incredible story but he looked such a wild, romantic figure, with his Russian leather boots of which he was inordinately proud, that I was half inclined to believe him.

It was a long walk back to Sangana and by the time Masud appeared to see his film it was late. Charles had patched up the broken reel and amazingly it worked, although the sound was poor.

In yet another attempt to get all our bags in one place, Tom had left at eight o'clock to drive to Shawa, and did not return until 10.30. He reported that some of the equipment had been taken up to the *qarârgâh* a couple of miles from the road and so he had had to climb up there in the dark to retrieve it. I was extremely impressed by, and grateful for, his energy and enthusiasm.

We got to bed very late and were woken early by a group of importunate mujahideen, who wanted us to film them singing before they set off for home. Mr Ali explained that Masud had left instructions for us to do this before following him to Shawa. (He had gone again, without warning. I doubted if he ever spent more than two nights in the same place.) Furious at being bulldozed like this, I tried to insist on having breakfast first, but failed. The four mujahideen, including Abdul Sattar, the mine expert, sang a series of songs, all of which sounded equally uninspiring, and we eventually used none of them.

Around mid-morning all the men of the village started to make for an open space under the trees. They were going to pray, this being a holiday, the Id e Qorban (Feast of the Servant of God), which celebrates Abraham's willingness to sacrifice his son Isaac. Our host slaughtered the sacrificial goat right under our window. Hearing the beast's piteous screams, I looked out in time to see the knife going in and the vermilion blood running across the dusty courtyard. As it expired, the goat turned its infinitely pathetic yellow eyes up at me in mute appeal. I turned away impotently, feeling diminished and demoralized by man's need to inflict death on so many other creatures.

The prayers lasted a good hour and at the end all two hundred or so men turned and embraced their neighbours, shaking hands and kissing one another on both cheeks. There were some wonderful-looking old men, all dressed in their best silken cloaks and turbans, their beards waggling as they greeted one another. One old fellow, with a skin like parchment, was said to be a hundred. Afterwards everyone had lunch, the men in the mosque, we in the isolation of our increasingly squalid upper room.

Later we packed everything up, ready to depart, and waited for the jeep, which finally came at three. Tom and I went ahead with half the equipment, driving up to Shawa in about twenty minutes, a journey that would have taken us two hours and much sweat on foot. We passed Do Ab for the last time, leaving on our left the green and white flags of the ancient graveyard fluttering stiffly in the breeze, and on our right the Darra.

Masud had absolutely refused to let us return the same way we had come, saying the route was now too dangerous, because of the Russians and hostile Hisbe groups in the border area. The Hisbe were led by a man called Gulbuddin who was Masud's arch enemy and, Masud claimed, in league with the Russians. As an example of their perfidy, he cited the case of the Russians who surprised and killed the twenty mujahideen at Shawa. They had been able to infiltrate the area, Masud said, because the local Hisbe had evacuated their village without telling Masud's men, leaving the way open for the Russians.

At Shawa, where the bridge was down, we had to unload the jeep and carry everything over to the other side where, to our joy, a lorry was waiting on Masud's instructions to take us to Zinneh. The jeep then went back for the others but kept breaking down and they did not arrive, having walked half the way, until five. We got to Zinneh just before dark and met Masud walking down the road with a group of mujahideen, smiling and looking relaxed. In the evening, after dinner, Charles rigged up the portable generator and we showed them some of our rushes. Despite the small screen and inevitable scrappiness of the rushes, Masud and the mujahideen watched intently and then applauded.

Afterwards, I made a little speech and presented the portable generator to Masud, explaining that it was very versatile, and could be used to charge car batteries or light up a small hospital. We then had a last talk about our journey back. Masud, with his customary decisiveness, said we would have to go through Nuristan, which meant carrying on up the Panjsher to Dasht-i-Riwat and Paryan, where we would get horses. He admitted it was a long, high route but made light of the difficulties, saying that although he had never used it himself, the path was by now relatively well-worn. (This turned out to be the joke of the expedition.)

'How long will it take?' we asked him.

'Oh, about twelve days,' he replied nonchalantly.

Finally, conscious this would be our last conversation together, I asked him about himself, and how he had learnt about guerrilla warfare. He said that when in exile in Pakistan in the late seventies he had read a great deal – Mao Tse tung, Che Guevara, Régis Debray, the French left-winger, and an American general whose name he had forgotten.

'The American book was the best of all,' Masud declared. It sounded as if it had been a text book on counter-insurgency for the American Special Forces. But apart from the American general, he considered that Mao was the best teacher: '*Le livre de Mao, il est très, très bon!*' Masud also explained how his guerrilla movement was based around twenty *qarârgâhs* in the Panjsher. Each *qarârgâh* had a group of about thirty mujahideen for self-defence, rather like a Home Guard, and another mobile group of thirty – a strike force that could operate anywhere inside or outside the Panjsher. In turn each *qarârgâh* was divided into political, military, economic, law and health sections, and each had a council of ten elected villagers to advise the Commander.

The valley itself, he explained, was highly organized, with himself as overall military and political leader. Abdul Hai was his second-in-command and below them were a number of departments which sounded like embryo ministries: military, economic, law, culture and information, political, health, intelligence and Kabul affairs. The Kabul section was subdivided into military affairs (very important and top secret, Masud said), student affairs and propaganda – newspapers and leaflets. Kabul was also vital from an economic point of view, since Masud levied a war tax of five per cent on the earnings of all Panjsheris in the capital. There was little doubt in my mind that everyone had to pay. Finally, Masud said that he had had no fresh supplies of arms or ammunition during the last offensive – the Hisbe had blocked all his convoys.

Next morning we were up early, excited by the prospect of finally starting our return journey. It was Tuesday, 28 September, our forty-ninth day in Afghanistan.

Just before we climbed aboard the lorry which was to take us to Dasht-i-Riwat, I saw Masud pacing up and down alone, deep in thought, and went to speak to him. I said I would report what was happening to the outside world and he asked me if I would see President Zia of Pakistan. I said I would make every effort to see him. (I failed. Zia was in China.)

'Should I tell him how the Pakistanis are stealing your new weapons and substituting old guns?'

Without hesitation, Masud nodded. 'Yes, tell him.'

As we drove off Masud stood in the middle of the road, waving goodbye, his eagle's face lit by a wide smile, and then he walked away with his springy, slightly crouching step. It was our last view of him.

After so much walking, it was a luxury to sit in relative comfort while the lorry rattled across the same countryside we had trekked through with such effort. At Khenj we got out to stretch our legs and have a cup of tea. There was no sign of the thumbless Jamil: someone said he was off on another convoy mission, but the old man who claimed to have killed eight Russians was there and joined us for tea, showing off his 303 and his tooled leather boots. Afghans seem to be always on the move, hitching a lift when they can, but usually travelling on foot, sleeping and eating with family or friends.

Further on, we came across a yoke of oxen threshing maize and banged on the top of the cab for the lorry to stop. Charles and Tom jumped down and started filming. It was a perfect scene: the soft morning light, the team of oxen yoked tightly together, their heads low as they went round and round trampling the golden stalks, the farmers laughing and joking at the idea of being filmed. Behind them the north wall of the Panjsher towered into the blue sky, the peaks white with new snow.

Just as we were about to leave, there was a frightening roar and two Russian jets swept over our heads. Everyone immediately leaped into action, the gear was stowed and the lorry started in a matter of seconds. We were all conscious that if the Russians had seen us they might well come back and shoot us up. A lorryload of people was a tempting target. We lurched off at top speed down the road for a mile or so, only slowing down near the river where the road was shielded by the steep hillside. There we halted and waited. A quarter of an hour later, one jet came back, fairly high, and went on. The Russian pilots either had not seen us or were not interested and we drove on, reaching Dasht-i-Riwat at lunchtime, where we were met by a friendly, local Commander. After a very good lunch of rice, mutton, *mast* and fruit we were taken off to see the local prison. We walked the length of the village and across the river. At this point the Commander and his men became very excited, pointing at the Panjsher below.

'What is it?' I demanded.

'The colour of the water,' Stéphane explained. 'They say the Russian planes that flew up the valley yesterday dropped something in the water.'

We all stared at the river, two hundred feet below us and agreed it did look exceptionally green. We asked what they thought the Russians had dropped and Stéphane questioned the Commander.

'They don't know, but they say the water is a different colour and have heard that two cows died after drinking from the river.'

'We would like to get a shot of them. Will they tell us where they are?'

Stéphane nodded, 'Of course.'

We walked down to the river, taking several shots contrasting its greenness with the very normal-looking irrigation channel beside it. Further up, where we had to cross by a narrow bridge, the river made a deep pool. The water looked glassy green. While Charles was taking a shot of it, I noticed that the Commander was on the far bank, filling a bottle with water. I could not be absolutely sure, but it seemed to me he had taken it from just below the point where another stream joined the Panjsher and where the water was noticeably less green. (We later transported this precious sample all the way back to London, where it was analysed and found to be non-toxic, although full of bacteria. We never saw the dead cows, either.)

We followed a narrow gorge for a mile or so, suddenly emerging in a natural amphitheatre. On the far side, blending beautifully with its surroundings, was a stone fort surrounded by crags, on the top of which were two or three mujahideen machine-gun posts. The Commander led the way through the low, narrow outer door. Inside, the prisoners were drawn up in two rows, ordinary prisoners-of-war on the left, political prisoners on the right. Among the latter was a furtive, pock-marked man wearing a white, knitted skull cap. He was, the mujahideen proudly explained, a senior political Commissar in the Afghan Army who had been captured near Rokha.

I tried to interview him in English, but it was an uphill struggle linguistically as well as journalistically. Naturally he was careful not to say anything that might incriminate him even more, if that were possible, with his captors. Since he persisted in saying that he had deserted, when we had been told he had been captured, I doubted he would tell the truth about anything. Nevertheless, I asked him if, now he had seen the mujahideen for himself, he still believed they were a mere handful of bandits.

'No,' he said, 'now I have met the mujahideen, I know they are patriots and have the support of the people of Afghanistan.' Our mujahid escort and the Commander glowered at him menacingly and kept interrupting. I was not surprised the Commissar began to sweat.

'How do the Russians see the war now?' I asked.

They had originally thought it would not take them very long to defeat the mujahideen, he said, but now they were not so sure. They were suffering casualties and were much more pessimistic. I watched him as he twisted and turned, trying to benefit from the occasion, but terrified he would say the wrong thing and destroy himself.

He told me he had been in the Afghan Army for seventeen years. I doubted if he would ever see Kabul again, but the Commander told us that the ordinary military prisoners would be released in a few days' time and sent home; indeed a few days later one of them arrived at the house where we were staying, apparently a free man. Since most of them were press-ganged into the Army in the first place, I guessed the majority would end up in the mujahideen.

As we were about to leave, a tall young man was brought in, dressed in a Russian peaked cap. He turned out to be a twenty-year-old Turkman from Tashkent, who had deserted to the mujahideen. He was not a prisoner, he said, and had just come back from Nuristan where Masud had sent him to learn about Islam. There are forty-five million Muslims in the southern states of the Soviet Union – Turkmenistan, Uzbekistan and Tadjikistan – and young Abdullah Oaf was one of them. It must have taken a lot of courage to desert from his unit and give himself up to the mujahideen. He had undoubtedly been helped by the fact that he spoke Farsi. I asked him if there were many more Muslims in the Soviet Union who were equally interested in Islam and he said there were, but they did not understand what was going on in Afghanistan.

'The Commanders tell them the Americans are here . . . they think they are coming to fight the Americans.'

Abdullah Oaf seemed to me to be an essentially tragic figure. He could never return to the Soviet Union, and never see his family or friends again. He had, for whatever reason, crossed his own particular Rubicon and there was no going back.

That evening we dined with some of the Dasht-i-Riwat emerald dealers. That may sound very grand but in reality all it meant was three or four averagely villainous-looking men came into our room, shook hands, and were eventually offered food by the Commander.

Through Stéphane he asked if we would like to see some emeralds. We all said we would and the shabbiest-looking Afghan hitched up his shirt, producing a small wad of tissue paper, which he unwrapped carefully to reveal fifteen or twenty emeralds. The smallest was the size of a seed pearl and the biggest not much larger than a pea, but rectangular.

'How much is that worth?'

'Seventy thousand Afghanis.'

'Why, that's £7,000!' I was amazed.

'Do you want to buy it?'

'Er, thank you very much, not at the moment. We are not carrying all that much money.' After everyone had examined the emeralds in turn, squirming about on the floor to do so, the inscrutable dealer wrapped his stones in their tissue paper and stowed them away in the voluminous folds of his nether garments.

The emeralds, which are found in certain rock formations in the mountains round Dasht-i-Riwat, used to be auctioned in the town.

But because of the war, they are now exported to Pakistan, where dealers come from far and wide, especially Germany, to buy them. Ten per cent of all sales is paid over to Masud's organization. He had told us himself how important the sale of emeralds was to his war effort.

After the emeralds, we had another surprise. A handsome fellow came into the room and smilingly asked in English, 'Are you British?'

'Yes,' we chorused. 'Who are you?'

'My name is Semad Mir and I am a hunter.'

'What do you hunt?'

'Marco Polo sheep.'

We were momentarily confused. The Marco Polo sheep we discovered, is a huge wild sheep found only in the Pamirs, an extremely high mountain range that straddles the border between Afghanistan, China and the Soviet Union. In normal times, Semad Mir explained, you would get there via the Wakhan Corridor, a narrow spit of Afghan territory that juts out to the east and is bordered by the Soviet Union to the north, China to the east and Pakistan to the south.

'Can you still go there?' I asked, although I already knew the answer.

'No,' he answered gloomily, 'the Russians now control the Wakhan. You cannot go there any more to hunt the Marco Polo sheep.'

In the old days, he said, he had often taken one of the Rothschilds to the Wakhan: like big-game hunting in Africa, a licence was required to shoot, and at $17,000 a sheep, the three-week trip must have been rather expensive.

'Have you ever seen a Marco Polo sheep?' Semad Mir asked. We all shook our heads.

'I have a pair of horns at home,' he said. 'I will fetch them.' They were huge, heavy and curling and I could quite believe that a full-grown sheep stood five feet at the shoulder. I wondered if the Russians were shooting them now.

The next stage of the journey was to Paryan, at the head of the valley, where we would branch off to Nuristan. Horses and guides would arrive in the morning, the Commander promised. It all seemed too good to be true.

14

Next morning Stéphane and I went into the village to buy rice, sugar, tea, potatoes, onions and salt for the journey, while Nigel negotiated with the horsemen. He soon discovered that the arrangements he made the night before had now changed. Instead of taking us to Pakistan, they were prepared to go only as far as Paryan, fifteen miles away, and for that they wanted one thousand Afghanis (£10) each, which we discovered later was three times what it should have cost. Not having any alternative, we had to agree. Buying provisions for the twelve-day crossing of Nuristan and loading them took most of the morning and it was noon by the time we set off with six horses.

Above Dasht-i-Riwat the valley narrowed and the track ran along the side of the mountain, often high above the river. The landscape was startlingly beautiful, the river glowing emerald-green in the deeper pools. I could not make up my mind if the Russians really had dropped anything in it. Before long, our little convoy became hopelessly spread out, most of the horsemen being miles in front while we slogged along on foot at the back, taking it in turns to ride our only saddle horse. Half-way to Paryan, we came on Tom, waiting for us by a stone hut beside the track.

'They want us to have some *chai*,' he announced. There were weary shouts of approval and we ducked through the narrow doorway. Inside, as our eyes became accustomed to the gloom, we saw that, apart from the usual carpets on the floor, the men occupying this herdsman's shelter had brought most of their belongings with them. One thing in particular caught our eye; a striped garment on a shelf.

The owner obligingly fetched it down and unfolded it. It was a long, striped silk cloak and we all admired it.

'He says you can have it if you want. He will give it to you for the same money as he paid – twenty-five hundred Afghanis, (£25). He bought it in Andarab for his wedding, but he says he will get another,' Stéphane explained. I was amazed at the man's generosity.

'I'll buy it from him,' Nigel said swiftly and with a charming smile, the young bridegroom-to-be pushed it into his hands. It was hand-sewn, with long sleeves and as multi-coloured as Joseph's coat. I could not suppress a pang of envy; I too would have liked it, totally impractical as it was.

The narrow valley suddenly widened and we found ourselves looking at a sweep of upland meadow with several villages dotted across it, smoke from the cooking fires rising into the still, evening air. At the end of the day's march, this remote sunlit valley looked wonderfully welcoming.

Like so many Afghan villages, Paryan is enormously spread out, consisting of several hamlets stretching over miles, and it was not until after dark that we finally reached the *qarârgâh*, slipping and stumbling down a steep slope in the dark. The horsemen had dumped our equipment and disappeared. The local mujahideen told us the Commander was away but expected him back tomorrow, so we unrolled our sleeping bags in the cramped and dirty-looking space available and, after a few mouthfuls of rice, were quickly asleep.

Next morning, the beauty of our surroundings was fully revealed. Our farmhouse stood above a mill stream and a green meadow, with the Panjsher River just beyond. On the far bank, the fields sloped up to a fair-sized hamlet of solidly-built timber and mud houses, and in the distance, the mountains rose forbiddingly into the pale blue sky, the peaks iced with snow. My heart sank slightly as I gazed at them. Somehow, on our way out, we would have to climb them, and even bigger mountains.

After breakfast Charles, Tom and I set off to film the villagers threshing maize, the yoked oxen turning round and round in a tight circle, their hooves trampling the maize stalks into chaff. A woman with a little boy at her side was threshing wheat by hand, pounding the stalks with a stick. Further on, men were bagging beans and humping them up the hill. I felt, as I did many times in Afghanistan, that I was looking at a scene from the Middle Ages, in which there

Paryan: weighing out 303 ammunition, just arrived by arms convoy from Nuristan. It was probably Second World War vintage (previous page)

Nuristan: the highest and most beautiful part of Afghanistan. Our route took us over five passes of up to 15,000 feet

Our guides: Nur (left) and Rahman. Rahman tried to attack Tom with a stone and had to be forcibly restrained (inset)

The camera horse went for a drink and nearly drowned, soaking the camera in the process. Miraculously it still worked (above)

Our best horse. He carried our heaviest gear up and down the mountains of Nuristan for nearly 200 miles (below)

Crossing Chamar Pass – I lead my reluctant chestnut over the top. On the second pass, two horses fell (right)

The koffi at Peshawarak. We slept in the room on the left, the object of intense local interest (overleaf)

The author trying his hand at golf, Nuristan-style, beside the mosque at Pul-i-Rostan. The local boys played better (above)

Working on my script on the roof at Sangana. At this point I doubted if the documentary would ever be made (below)

were no machines; everything was done by hand. The cries of the
men driving the oxen, the grunts as the others hoisted the great bags
of beans onto their backs and tramped off across the meadow to the
houses above, the murmur of the river, the high-pitched voices of the
children, the dying heat of the autumnal sun, the purity of the air
here, at ten thousand feet, made one word irresistibly spring to mind:
idyllic.

Suddenly and totally unexpectedly, two Sukhoy bombers went
right over our heads, already past us before we heard their roar.
They banked slightly to follow the curve of the valley and
disappeared. Immediately, the mood changed as if a cloud had
covered the sun.

'They will come back,' an Afghan said.

'When?'

'*Nim szad, nim szad.*' In half an hour.

We were waiting for them when they returned, twenty minutes
later, and although the camera was ready to film, they came so fast
that we nearly missed them again. They hurtled past in formation,
their jet noise shattering the peace of the valley and reverberating
menacingly off the mountains. I guessed the intention was partly
routine patrol, partly intimidation.

Next day, 1 October, our fifty-second day in Afghanistan, I wrote
in my diary:

My birthday. Fifty-five to Heaven. I thank God that I am so fit and happy. I
don't feel my age. Maybe I look it though. Some Afghan told me last night
his turban (very smelly) suited me and Stéphane said, 'Yes, it is good for
white hair!'

I got up at six and went outside to wash in the stream below the
house. The horses were supposed to come at 6.30, but needless to say
they did not. Instead, a man brought a basketful of delicious fresh
rolls, which we had ordered specially for the journey. The rest of the
day was spent waiting for the horses to arrive and arguing with our
guide, a rough-looking, hunch-backed individual called Rahman,
about how many bags his horse should carry. Because the Nuristan
route was known to be long and arduous, we had decided each of us
should have a horse to ride – and carry our personal kit – and that we
would need three pack horses. The Commander, who had arrived
overnight, explained that at the moment it was difficult to find any
horses at all, because they had just sent five hundred to Pakistan to

bring in arms. Even allowing for Afghan exaggeration, this was bad news.

Leaving Nigel and Stéphane to worry about the horses, I retired to the roof to read. Below me, the river resembled the River Dee at Balmoral, where I grew up. The willows were beginning to turn gold, just like the silver birches on Deeside, and by some odd trick of light the mountain beyond looked as if it was covered in heather. The whole scene reminded me so strongly of Scotland that I felt quite homesick. It must have been the effect of my birthday.

There was a brilliant full moon when we went to bed, but overnight the weather changed dramatically. We woke to find it was pouring with rain in the valley and snow had fallen on the higher ground. The realization that the high passes of Nuristan would already be under snow was both depressing and disturbing. It would be no joke to be trapped in Afghanistan for the winter and to add to our troubles, the scowling Rahman arrived to say that his horse was lame. The conversation now took a dizzy turn, with Rahman arguing that the route through Nuristan was too dangerous; the last convoy had lost four horses out of twenty-five. It would be better for all concerned, he added, if we were to revert to our original plan and leave via the Koh-i-Safi. Since this was at least a devil we knew, we promptly took up the suggestion and asked the Commander if Tom and Stéphane should not set off immediately to get Masud's approval, while Nigel, Charles and I followed with the equipment.

Seeing that we were serious, the Commander, who Stéphane said was a close friend of Masud's, got cold feet. He could not seriously contemplate countermanding Masud's orders, and they were that we should leave by Nuristan. After more discussion, made long and tedious by the fact that Stéphane had to translate every exchange, the Commander announced that the Nuristan route was all right after all.

Determined to get as many opinions as possible, I asked the man who had insisted I try on his smelly turban if he thought it was a practical route. He turned out to be Commander of Koran Monjan, a staging post much higher up on the traditional route to Pakistan, which had been captured by the Russians and the Afghan army. He grinned encouragingly. '*Inshallah*' (God willing) was all he said.

But even if our route was decided, we were still short of our target of eight horses, and after more fruitless discussion, I suddenly lost my temper.

'*Birram,*' (Let's go) I shouted. '*Birram, birram,* then for God's sake.'

My outburst may have been embarrassing, but at least it galvanized everyone into action, including the Commander. He was suddenly at pains to assure us that the horses would be here in '*yak szad*' (one hour). This proved over-optimistic and it was nearly dark when the mullah, who had been commissioned to scour the countryside for horses, returned with three more animals. We were now up to seven, only one short, and the eighth, we were told, was only an hour away up the valley. We would collect it on our way through in the morning. We were once again on the verge of departure and everyone's spirits, which had sunk very low, rose again.

I was impatient to get off early, but the loading seemed to be an endless business and we finally did not leave the *qarârgâh* until ten. Once on the move, however, all the irritation and frustration of the past few days dropped away and I gazed eagerly around the valley. Everywhere the country basked in brilliant sunshine and men were bringing in the harvest from their tiny stone-walled fields, the tops of the houses already heaped high with winter fodder for their animals.

We desperately needed pictures of refugees and the Commander, cantering beside us on his handsome grey stallion, said we would find some at the last village. He was right. As we dismounted in a field by the village, I noticed a group of children on the far side of the river. They were standing in front of a cave, motionless, staring in our direction.

'Refugees?' I asked.

The Commander nodded. We unpacked the camera, always a tedious business as it meant unloading the horse first, and started to film. The refugees simply stood and looked at us, from across the valley, as if they inhabited another planet. All filming is a laborious task and to get close-ups we had to dismantle the tripod, unclamp the camera and carry everything, as well as the recorder, through the village, down the hill and over a bridge to the other side. On the way we passed three women sitting at the mouth of a small cave. Inside, a rifle leaned against the rock; that and a big tin pot to fetch water from the river seemed to be their only possessions. Rahman said they came from Bazarak. A number had found lodging in the village but some had had to make do with the rocks. Three small children squatted against the cliff, watching us intently as we worked. The smallest child seemed to be eating earth – dipping her finger in the dust and then pretending to lick it. I suppose it was a game, but, remembering what Jean-Philippe had said about psychological illness, I wondered if this particular child was suffering from a nervous tic.

As we rode out of the village we lost the Commander and Stéphane and struggled on alone with Rahman, climbing to a village perched high on a hill, from where we had a fascinating view. The valley at this point made a rough 'Y' and a tiny village nestled in the fork, protected by a small, steep, rocky hill. In the evening light, surrounded by its wheatfields, with the sheaves drawn up in neat rows, it reminded me of the model farm I had played with as a boy.

We rode on, with the sun on our backs, towards Chamar. It was even more imposing, a cluster of houses, like a fortress, perched on the edge of the hill, high above a rushing stream. Men and horses milled about in front of the massive walls as our equipment was unpacked and sorted into fresh loads for the journey next day. Our eighth horse was waiting; a fine, sturdy, dark bay with an intelligent head, easily the best of a rather sorry lot. Our second guide, Nur, also made his first appearance. He seemed friendly and capable, and was greeted by Rahman like a long-lost brother.

We eventually adjourned to a big, upstairs room full of mujahideen, who were noisily counting out hundreds of rounds of old 303 ammunition and occasionally dropping RPG7 rockets on the floor. The Commander and his friend from Koran Monjan left us and rode back to Paryan in the dark, and after our rice we settled down to get what sleep we could. We had been promised an early start.

It was extremely early. We were up at two, spent two hours and much debate loading the horses, and left at four. Judas Iscariot, as Nigel had nicknamed Rahman, became exceedingly angry when I did not untie my horse but waited, rather indolently, for someone to do it for me. He shouted at me in Farsi, rather like a colonial Englishman shouting at a non-comprehending native. It was quite interesting to experience the process in reverse.

The cold was intense – we all wore thick gloves – but the moonlight made the going easier. I rode the new horse and he picked his way unerringly up the stony track, moving so quickly that he kept bumping into Judas-Rahman, who turned round and snarled at me to keep my distance. We had one mujahid from Chamar with us, armed with a 303, as escort.

Dawn came at six, lighting the peaks in front of and behind us with a delicate, rosy pink. I had noticed pale patches on the side of the mountain and now daylight revealed that they were unharvested wheatfields, improbable as that might seem at the beginning of October. At eight we reached a rough shelter made of huge slabs of rock and managed, after coaxing a fire out of damp bits of bushes, to boil our kettle and make tea.

We set off again at ten, Nur, Rahman and the mujahid walking, the rest of us riding. It was a long pull up the valley with Mir Samir, 19,880 feet, now visible on our right. As we drew closer we could see what a huge, forbidding mountain it was, with its great rock buttresses and snowy moraines, the summit lost in cloud. We bore left, climbed to a plateau and found ourselves confronting the Chamar Pass, the first of five that we had been told lay between us and Pakistan. It was a daunting sight, the route zigzagging right up the almost vertical face of the mountain.

We started up, pulling our horses behind us. Mine went up like a deer and I found the climb slightly easier than I had expected (we were all of course much fitter now); we reached the top at two, much more quickly than I would have thought possible. Just as we looked back from the ridge, the clouds that had covered Mir Samir all day lifted and it stood forth in all its majesty, an almost perfect snow-capped pyramid. To the south, a series of ridges fell away, as jagged as a hacksaw blade.

Going down was as difficult and more dangerous, for the north-east face was icy, and the horses slipped and stumbled in alarming fashion, cutting their fetlocks on the sharp stones and leaving patches of blood on the trail. Rahman and Nur, I noticed, helped the heavily-loaded horses to negotiate the steepest sections by grabbing their tails and acting rather like anchor men in a tug-of-war team. To make them go faster, they shouted what sounded like '*chu, chu. . . .*'

At one point the stench of decomposing matter assailed our nostrils and we passed the carcase of a dead horse, (the first of many) which had either broken a leg and been left to die, or simply not had the strength to climb the final stretch. There was a rush of wings and I looked up, startled, to see the great yellow-chested, bearded lammergeier go sailing past, an interested observer of our progress. Far below, we could see a green valley beckoning us, but it took two hours of heel-jarring descent before we reached it. We then followed a lovely, shingly stream, its water as clear as crystal.

When the stream broadened, we dismounted to cross by some boulders and just as I reached the far side I heard a cry and turned to see Tom sprawling in the water by the far bank. Nur, who was half-way across, turned immediately and I followed. Together we carried him back to the bank; he had slipped, hitting his head on a rock, and almost knocked himself out. He lay on the grass groaning for several minutes, but finally sat up and after a rest, was able to walk the remaining mile to a stone bothy where we were to spend the night. Just before we arrived all the bags slipped off my horse and Nur had to come to the rescue again.

Tom had a splitting headache so I made him get into his sleeping bag, gave him a couple of pain killers and he was fast asleep before supper. But he did not miss much; even Rahman and Nur were unable to make a big enough fire to cook rice, so we dined instead off wheat biscuits, raisins, Kendal Mint Cake and copious draughts of tea. It tasted better than any wine.

We all bedded down in the tiny hut, Tom, myself, Nigel and Stéphane in a row, with Charles across our feet at the bottom. He was impeded slightly by a mound of dried cow dung, which is used as fuel. Before getting into his sleeping bag, Stéphane de-loused himself with my insect powder. You could see lice quite clearly on his blue vest, big fat specimens which he thought he had picked up from the communal bedding at the Paryan *qarârgâh*. It proved the point, for me at any rate, that one's own sleeping bag, judiciously sprinkled with powder, is the best protection against the multifarious denizens of the Afghan outback.

By Afghan standards, next morning was a lazy one. We rose at 6.30 and had tea and hard biscuits at seven. Loading took a long time (Rahman and Nur complaining that getting eight horses ready was too much for two men), and we did not leave until 9.30. Our mujahid escort, having got us over the Chamar Pass, shook hands and departed for home, an indescribably lonely figure as he marched off up the valley.

Rahman said we would reach the first village in Nuristan at lunchtime, but infuriatingly, although not surprisingly, this turned out to be wildly optimistic. The track became very rough and the valley scored by huge moraines, the litter of boulders, some as big as houses, left behind by glaciers. The horses had to pick their way painfully, opening the cuts on their legs and inflicting new ones. I began to realize that most of our horses were in poor condition – the crafty Afghan farmers of Paryan had sold us their most worthless beasts. Rahman had removed my dark bay, loading him up with the heaviest camera equipment, and had given me instead a gangling, stumbling chestnut who had to be driven along with a stick and frequent shouts of '*Chu.*'

Stopping only to drink tea with twenty or thirty mujahideen who were on their way from Badakhshan in the north to Pakistan for arms, we walked and rode all day, reaching the promised village at five. It turned out to be another, larger stone bothy with 'restaurant' attached, where an evil-looking Nuristani, with sharp, ferrety features, promised us dinner. The place itself was enchanting, a green meadow at the confluence of two rivers, surrounded by small trees – silver birches, willows and wild briars, some already turning scarlet. At the end of the valley a towering massif shut off the view to the south: we were looking at the roof of Afghanistan.

Stéphane ingratiated himself with the evil-looking owner and we sat in his hovel, our eyes smarting from the wood smoke until dinner was finally ready. It was filthy, tough goat and tepid tea, which was not improved by having to be carried to the hut in a gale. During the night it rained heavily, which meant it was snowing higher up. In the morning the ferrety Nuristani tried to overcharge us outrageously: Stéphane managed to beat him down in the end, but it was a warning that, unlike the Panjsheris, the Nuristanis were out to get as much as possible from luckless travellers.

Nigel, as the purse-holder, was already worried about mounting costs. On the way in we had paid only for the hire of four horses. Now we had bought or rented eight and we also had to pay for their feed and our own food. To leave us with as much cash as possible, the Paryan Commander had obligingly agreed to let us pay half what we owed for the horses in Pakistan. Even then, we were only just going to have enough.

The new snow glinted on the mountain tops as we rode off up the side valley and Nigel exclaimed that he felt like John Wayne for the first half hour; after that the rigours of the trail tended to obliterate the first fine careless rapture. The river tumbled and foamed beside the path as, accompanied by the mujahideen from Badakhshan, we climbed up through groves of silver birch towards the formidable wall of snow-covered mountains ahead of us. We halted at two, on a barren upland and a long discussion ensued with Rahman, Nur and the mujahideen about our tactics for crossing the next big pass. First,

Rahman said we should sleep where we were, in the open, and set off in the early hours. Then, after conferring with some mujahideen who had just crossed the pass and said it had taken them ten or twelve hours, he decided we should leave at 8.00 p.m. Doubt now crept in as to whether there were one or two passes and in the end, Rahman and Nur – a case of the blind leading the blind – announced that we would leave at ten.

One or two of us demurred at the thought of crossing the pass in the middle of the night, but Rahman argued that only by doing so could we hope to reach the next village, which was a long way beyond the pass, in daylight. Since we felt that he should know best, we reluctantly agreed. That settled, our thoughts turned to food.

'I'll make some soup,' Nigel said, 'if someone will make a fire and fetch some water.' Search parties immediately set off to gather fuel – clumps of a prickly bush which we tore up by the roots. It flared up quickly and then spluttered and smouldered giving off clouds of smoke. After lengthy preparations Nigel finally produced two cupfuls each of hot lentil soup which we drank thirstily in a flurry of snow. It became noticeably colder, although we were all wearing everything we had: thermal underwear, two sweaters, cagoule, balaclava and heavy gloves. Rahman and Nur, undeterred by the conditions, were in a good mood, singing Panjsheri songs at the tops of their voices as the snowflakes hissed on the fire. Judas in particular had a good voice.

Despite thick socks and heavy Timberland boots, my feet were so cold that it was a relief when at ten we left the shelter of our rock and set off in the darkness. With no moon and little idea of where he was going, Rahman promptly lost the way, leading us into a maze of rocks from which there was no exit. I argued that the path must lie beside the river and, followed by Nur, clambered down over a jumble of rocks to find it, a pale streak among the shadows. The moon was still hidden by the mountain on our left, but ahead of us the higher slopes were ghostly white.

We now crossed a huge bowl, the horses skidding on the flat icy rocks, and came to the foot of a great snowy wall. This was the pass and high above us, in the now bright moonlight, it looked impossibly difficult.

We started, first traversing a long, slippery slope, and then zigzagging up the icy path, the horses fighting to keep their feet. The last stretch was very dangerous, the cliff wall rising sheer on the left and dropping away almost as sharply on the right. Tom, Charles, Nigel and I reached the top and walked round the corner to the other side, from where we looked down on a great amphitheatre of mountains surrounded by a rim of icy peaks. It was a scene of awesome splendour. We had been waiting, for perhaps ten minutes, when I suddenly wondered what had happened to the others. I got up and walked back round the corner. After a second or two I made out the figure of Stéphane standing forty or fifty feet below me in the shadow. A horse, still loaded, stood at the top of the path.

'Are you all right?' I shouted.

'Two of the horses have fallen,' he shouted back. 'It's a miracle that they aren't dead.'

I peered down and saw a horse standing, stiff with fright, on a narrow ledge twenty feet below the path. Rahman and Nur had unloaded it and were trying to get it to move, but the wretched animal refused to budge.

'I'll get the others,' I said urgently, catching hold of the horse beside me and, not realizing it was the other casualty, led it round to where the others were sitting.

'Quick,' I shouted, 'Tom, Charles, there's been an accident, two of the horses have fallen.' They got up at once and followed me round.

'Can you help get the equipment up?' Stéphane shouted. Charles and I edged our way carefully over the icy rocks and hauled it to safety, including the saddle bag with all our video tapes. We went back to see what was happening below. The horse still stood trembling on the ledge, Rahman and Nur beside it. Then, with one of them hauling on the reins, the other shoving from behind and both shouting encouragement, they finally managed to propel it off the ledge. For a second or two its hooves scrabbled desperately to get a grip on the side of the cliff and then with a terrific spring it cat-jumped up to the path and we all gave a cheer.

Stéphane climbed to meet us. 'The first horse fell ten or fifteen feet right on to its back. That's probably what saved its life. Have you seen the camera case? It's like a pancake. Then the second horse, which was below, also slipped and fell, making two somersaults. If Nur had not caught it by the hind legs when it was going over, it would certainly have fallen to its death. I don't know how he managed to stop it.' The strength of the Afghans never ceased to amaze me.

'Rahman is hurt,' Stéphane went on. 'He got a bad kick when he was trying to get the second horse up.' Rahman, however, gave no appearance of being badly hurt and he and Nur promptly loaded up the still-shivering horse and we started down.

The descent turned out to be a different sort of nightmare. The rocks were completely iced over and so slippery that I thought we would never get the frightened and exhausted animals down. After half an hour Charles's horse fell, catching its foot in a crack in the rock. It lay there, groaning, unable to get up, its head poking forward in a pathetic manner. Nur, Charles and I struggled desperately to get it up but, unable to free its hind leg, it kept falling back. Finally, Nur, by a remarkable combination of skill and strength, yanked the trapped hoof free and the horse staggered groggily to its feet. I was convinced from the way it had been groaning that it had broken a leg, but apart from a nasty cut it was perfectly sound.

Half-way down we stopped for a rest. It was now about four in the morning and to our amazement, and despite the fact that it was freezing cold, Rahman and Nur lay down on a flat rock and promptly went to sleep. After a quarter of an hour sitting shivering, we insisted on going on, although Nur and Rahman looked as if they would have happily slept for another hour.

We descended without further mishap, marching towards a magnificently fiery-red sky, which glowed like a furnace behind the peaks in front of us, eventually reaching a sunny meadow above a stream at around six. Some nomads were just striking camp to climb the pass, their goats and children running in front of them, the women carrying their pots and pans on their heads. We bought some milky yoghurt at an exorbitant price from one man, requisitioned one of their still smouldering fires and started to cook a brunch of rice, fried potatoes and onions.

I had a thorough wash, my first for weeks, in the ice-cold stream, and discovered several lice on my dark blue thermal underwear. (The experts recommend dark underwear to show up their white bodies.) Now more skilled at washing first the top half of my body and then the lower, without ever exposing the whole of myself, I emerged clean but aware of how painfully thin I had become. The sight of my skinny ribs and belly in Nigel's shaving mirror reminded me of the gruesome Fasting Buddha in the museum at Peshawar. But I felt extremely fit, the sun was warm on our backs, Tom and Stéphane's cooking was excellent, and we had conquered the second of our five big passes.

We left the meadow at noon, descended by easy stages to a broad valley where my horse, in his eagerness to drink, slipped his saddle and threw me over his head into the river. Two Nuristanis, who happened to be crossing, stood and watched in some amazement. One refused my signal for help but the other came leaping nimbly back and gave me a hand. Luckily Nur appeared in time to resaddle the brute. Afghan saddles are a law unto themselves, being held in place by a bewildering variety of leather thongs that I never succeeded in mastering.

A long, stony and, for me, uncomfortable ride down the valley followed, ending with a steep descent through a forest of pines. There followed a very arduous three-hour trek in the dark to the long-awaited village, during which my saddle slipped again while we were going up a steep hill, and I fell cursing among the bushes. We finally struggled into the village at nine and were shown into a particularly dirty and overcrowded room. I was so dog-tired I unrolled my sleeping bag and, ignoring the stares of our hosts, crawled into it without waiting for dinner. The others had chicken. Mine was left at my side, cold but still tasty, for breakfast in the morning.

15

The next day, before departing, we heard the strange tale of the people who lived in the house. They were outsiders from another valley and not very long before, a man had walked in, shot the owner and wounded two other people. They knew the murderer but, because he was a local and they were not, they had no redress. So they had to leave. The intricacies of the plot escaped me, but it struck me how very Afghan, not to say medieval, the story was.

Rahman came in to demand four hundred and fifty Afghanis for the horses' feed, which made Nigel, who was trying to keep to a daily budget of one thousand Afghanis (£10), blanch. We decided, however, that we should all eat as well as possible now, and go hungry, if necessary, later. To keep up our spirits we decided to have a sweep on the date we would reach Pakistan. It was the 8th so, being an optimist, I guessed the 15th; Tom the 16th; Charles the 17th; Stéphane the 18th; and Nigel, after some reluctance, the 19th.

As we rode off after breakfast, the track led through a series of gorges, the roughest bits forcing us to dismount and pick our way over the stones. Then, in the late afternoon, we emerged to see before us a great rock, with a cluster of houses clinging to one end and at the other, a high-walled building like a Crusader castle, or a lamasery in Tibet. Below it, a screen of trees glowed yellow in the sunshine and behind, a huge rounded mountain filled half the sky. We had arrived in the village of Kantiwar, on the river of the same name, on our fifth day out of Chamar. The village was in two halves, Lower and Upper, and we dismounted at Lower Kantiwar, in a little square shaded by tall trees. In one corner, the elders of the village reclined on a seat made from a hollowed-out tree trunk. Their thin foxy faces, long noses and deep-set eyes made them look very different from the Panjsheris.

The Nuristanis have an interesting history and are said to be descended from Alexander the Great's Macedonian soldiers. Certainly they were Christian until comparatively recently, being forcibly converted to Islam as late as the nineteenth century. Originally Nuristan was known as Kafiristan (to denote that its people were infidels), and had been a wine-growing country. Now, alas, it was as 'dry' as the rest of Afghanistan.

The *koffi*, an apology for a tea-house, on the other side of the square was shut, so we were shown to a leafy arbour complete with carpet next to the village cemetery. There we made camp and waited for tea, while the locals inspected our equipment with their usual irritating inquisitiveness.

A crisis now developed. The local *amir*, a sort of governor, was threatening to turn us back. Nigel and Stéphane departed hot-foot to placate him, returning the best part of two hours later to announce that the crisis had been averted; but only just. Initially he had refused to accept our letter from Masud requesting free passage and any assistance we might need, insisting that Masud had no authority and that we must have a letter from Professor Rabanni, the leader of the Jamiat. The only difficulty there, they explained, was that Rabanni was in Peshawar. Apparently only one group of foreigners had passed this way before and the *amir* suspected we were Russian spies.

However, the crisis averted, we dined, disappointingly as far as I was concerned, for I got only a small wing of chicken. Rahman and Nur, I noticed, usually came off best, Rahman having the infuriating habit of dividing up the portions with his fingers and keeping the best bits for himself. If we growled and grumbled too much, he would sulk and refuse to eat anything. Relations were beginning to deteriorate.

We left Kantiwar at six, climbing up past the deserted castle to the upper village, which turned out to be a cluster of houses clinging to the rock face like house-martins' nests, their balconies propped up by wooden pillars. There was some squabbling at this point and two mujahideen, who had said they would come with us to help with the horses, changed their minds and disappeared, making both Nur and Rahman extremely grumpy. Stéphane was also missing but we presumed he would soon catch us up, so we rode down the valley where they were harvesting the maize, the ripe cobs spread out to dry on the flat roofs, making creamy-orange splashes of colour among the trees.

Further on, huge cedars covered the rocky hillsides and in a clearing we saw our first log-cabin. I half expected to see a trapper in skins and a Davy Crockett hat, come out of the doorway and watch us ride past.

We then turned away from the river and started the long climb up through the cedars. Tom and the drivers started arguing about his horse, shouting at one another in a mixture of Farsi and English, until suddenly Nur and Rahman stalked off down the hill. Stéphane said they were so angry that they were threatening to go home. We waited, too exhausted to make a decision, and then luckily they reappeared and carried on, tight-lipped. They undoubtedly had a case: to get eight horses over these passes was too much for two men.

The altitude and general exhaustion were making us even rattier than usual and as we struggled on up the steep path, I found myself flying off the handle at Tom.

'I'm responsible for this expedition,' I shouted, 'I carry the can. Don't you forget it.'

Tom snapped back and we trudged on bad-temperedly. Luckily we now came to a sunlit meadow with a few large, log-built houses scattered across it.

'*Chai?*' we asked hopefully and they waved us on, grinning. Finally, in the last group of houses, beside a small stream, we found the local *koffi*. We were on a kind of ridge, the meadow sloping gently away in front of us; in the distance the mountains rose to an ice-capped wall. We dismounted outside the tea-house while the locals studied us intently. After apologizing to Tom, I said we should all keep a tight rein on our tempers and reminded everyone what a debt we owed to Stéphane. Without him, I said, our journey would have been almost impossible and at best a frightful experience.

The Mum Pass lay ahead, so, in an attempt to ease the tension, I decided it would be good for us to relax for the rest of the day. We would spend a lazy afternoon, have a good dinner and an early night. Mum was the most beautiful place we had yet seen. Its haunting Alpine quality, steep mountains covered with evergreens and houses built with great beams of timber, made me think of Haute Savoie, where we had spent a family skiing holiday the previous Christmas. We had a late chicken lunch and then Tom and Stéphane, our master chefs, cooked rice with raisins, onions and potatoes for dinner. Our host lit the stove and it burned all night, giving off a sweet smell of cedar wood. The room, with its massive door, solid window shutter (there was no glass in the window) and planked ceiling, all made of hand-hewn cedar, was the handsomest we had been in.

It was a morning of still and perfect beauty as we said goodbye and rode off across the meadow: Sunday, 10 October, our sixty-first day in Afghanistan. As we continued to climb through the tall cedars, a big bird, like a capercaillie, went shooting low over the tree-tops, closely pursued by a bigger bird. I saw a flash of talons, a predatory hunch of shoulder and reddish tail feathers fully extended. They made a terrific noise – *vooom* – as the larger bird, which I thought was an eagle, braked hard and seemed to be on the point of striking. The whole thing was over in a second, the trees concealing what must have been a sudden end.

We climbed steadily, stopping for a brief rest above the tree line, and then tackled the final ascent – or was it, as so often, a false crest? The foul smell of carrion came downwind; a dead horse lay somewhere among the tangle of rock. The night before I had been horrified when Nur showed me the sores on the backs of our horses, some of them badly infected. I had applied some disinfectant powder and dressings, but they really needed a massive dose of antibiotics and a complete rest.

A last steep pitch, the dry rocks giving a good grip, and to our surprise we stood at the top of the pass. It was only 9.30 and it had been much easier than we had expected, although admittedly conditions were perfect. While we were admiring the magnificent panorama on both sides of the ridge, I saw another huge bird with white wings sailing majestically along the valley below us. Stéphane said it was an Egyptian vulture. Going down was almost harder than the climb up, the path so steep in places that it was a wonder none of the horses fell. At one point, one of the loads got stuck in a cleft in the rocks and Nur and Rahman had to hammer and heave for half an hour to free the horse.

We came down to the valley through a tangle of fallen trees and found ourselves on the banks of a fast-flowing river. We had a local guide with us and, to save him getting his feet wet, I let him jump up behind me. His extra weight nearly brought us both to grief. My clumsy chestnut floundered about, almost falling twice. But I was

more concerned when the horse carrying the tapes (our whole film)
emerged with the saddle bags dripping wet. Charles and I unloaded
them at once, but they were well wrapped in plastic bags and Charles
was confident they had come to no harm. I insisted, however, on
unpacking them when we reached our destination that night.

We then headed roughly north up the valley. It was incredibly
beautiful; the ripeness of autumn in the air, the river plunging in a
crystal flood at our feet, huge cedars lining the path. After a time, the
valley broadened into a great meadow dotted with log cabins and at
the far end, the houses clinging dramatically to the side of the cliff, we
saw the village of Parun. As we reached the village a thunderstorm
broke in the mountains ahead, and we just had time to get the
equipment inside the mosque before the hailstones pelted down.
While we sank exhausted onto piles of hay, Stéphane went off to
scour the village for food. I noted in my diary: 'He is so clever and
willing. We are now at the half-way point. It seems a very long
business.' (In fact, I was wrong. We were well past half-way.)

After much discussion, an affable local persuaded us to eat at his
home. This meant taking our food up the rock face to his house
which, of course, was the highest in the village. One room was full of
local worthies but we were ushered into another, empty room and
after an hour or so an excellent dinner appeared: our own rice, our
host's chicken (for which we paid) and Nigel's select Fortnum's tea
to which they seemed to have helped themselves liberally. The only
thing that spoiled what would otherwise have been a delightful
evening was our host's dire warnings about the dreaded Papruk
Pass, two days' march away and by common consent the highest and
worst of the five. Our host said our equipment would have to be
portered up the last, very difficult stretch and we would need two
extra men, at three to four thousand Afghanis (£30–£40) each, to
help. This was an unexpected expense and would make an
irreparable hole in the budget. We went home in a sombre frame of
mind, sliding down the rock face in the dark, lit by the fitful glare of a
cedar torch.

It rained overnight and there was fresh snow on the mountains
next morning when I went for my constitutional. The latest report
was that it would take us two days to reach Papruk and we had still
found only one guide. Stéphane's horse, which had vanished
overnight, reappeared amid much sniggering and head-shaking.
According to Stéphane, it had been 'borrowed' by some local youths

to participate in what were described as 'perverted sexual practices'. On this note we left Parun and rode on up the valley, trotting as much as possible to make good time, past walnut trees shining bright yellow in the sun. We reached the last village at one and rode in through a big stone gateway, dismounting outside the mosque. For various reasons Rahman decided we should stop there and make an early start next morning, so we moved into the mosque and organized ourselves. The locals, who helped us make a fire in the middle of the big room, watched sympathetically as we started to cook the last of our soup. One old man, whom I had noticed on arrival, was particularly helpful. He had blue eyes and fair skin and, despite the raw cold, walked about quite cheerfully in his bare feet. I noticed too that his nose was large, red and bulbous, rather like a drinker's nose; a genetic memory, perhaps, of the days when Nuristanis were wine-drinkers. The soup was followed by delicious hot cheese which had to be scooped out of a bowl with bits of bread.

We went to bed at eight, knowing we would have to be up at 12.30. After the usual laborious loading process, we eventually set off at a quarter to three, making a brisk exit from the stone gate and climbing confidently up the hill. Within half an hour, our guides seemed to be lost and, after consulting a neighbouring farmer, we turned round cursing, and retraced our steps. I muttered to myself about the idiocy of tramping over the countryside in the dark when no one knew the way. We crossed the river, found the right path and made better progress over fairly easy ground.

At six, as it was getting light, we caught up with the mujahideen who had left before us and on whose help we were relying to cross the Papruk Pass. They were ensconced in two big stone huts, on the far side of the stream, brewing tea, the smoke from their fires rising invitingly in the cold morning air. We joined them, the mujahideen obligingly making room for us, and were handed cups of steaming green tea with lots of sugar.

Warmed and restored, we started the long climb at seven and shortly afterwards had to abandon Charles's horse. Although the going was easy, the horse suddenly came to a halt and refused to budge. Rahman eventually removed the saddle and left it to its fate. We had seen too many skeletons to doubt what that would be, but Rahman did tell the next group of mujahideen we passed that they could have the horse, so we hoped it would eventually find its way to the valley again. It seemed cruel to leave it on the side of the mountain, but the horse seemed quite unconcerned.

The route now turned sharply left and the real climb began. We passed three dead horses before reaching the snow line. Three or four inches of new snow had made the path slippery, so we proceeded more slowly. Pausing for breath, I looked up at what still had to be climbed: I estimated it to be several thousand feet, because the groups of mujahideen zigzagging along the face above us appeared as tiny dots moving very slowly. In fact, they were moving, as they always did, at a cracking pace, and with enough spare breath to chat to one another on the way. It was we who struggled upwards so painfully and slowly.

About five hundred feet from the top of the pass, the path became much steeper and rockier, a series of narrow, slippery zigzags. Two mujahideen waiting at the bottom of the rock face unloaded each horse, which was then manhandled up the track, one Afghan pulling its head and the other pushing from behind, twisting its tail to spur it on. Charles and I had been leading the horse carrying the video tapes in a big double saddle bag. After it had been unloaded and gone scrambling up the path, a mujahid, who did not look particularly strong, lifted the saddle bags, which must have weighed thirty or forty pounds, over his shoulder and strode off up the mountain as if he was carrying a feather duster.

While Charles and I wrestled with the camera up the steepest pitch and Nigel took photos from above, Tom's horse nearly went over the edge. Rahman and one of the mujahideen struggled furiously as the animal's hooves kept slipping. Suddenly it skated several yards backwards, Rahman hanging on to the reins like grim death and shouting at the top of his voice. They managed to stop it on the very edge. After a rest they tried again and this time the horse scrabbled its way to safety. The last stretch was a steep muddy chimney which turned out to be quite easy after the frozen snow and slippery rocks. At 12.30 we stood on the top of the Papruk Pass with a terrific sense of triumph. Everyone shook hands with everyone else, with Rahman, (even Rahman smiled), with Nur and the Commander of the mujahideen. When I thanked him profusely, he beamed with pleasure. Thank God for the Badakhshani mujahideen. We would never have done it without them.

Round us lay the most tremendous vista of snowy peaks, stretching range on range as far as the eye could see – I imagined to Chitral, our destination in Pakistan. It was brilliantly sunny up there at fifteen thousand feet, but the wind was bitterly cold and we moved fifty yards down the slope to where Tom was sitting.

Charles now produced a large bar of Kendal Mint Cake, which by some remarkable feat of self-denial he had carried all this way without devouring. With meticulous fairness he broke it into squares and passed them round. We wolfed them down with ecstatic cries of pleasure.

'It's just like frozen Crème de Menthe,' Nigel said, as if making an important discovery. He was right. With a little imagination we could be imbibing a swig of alcohol with every ambrosial mouthful. Lying there in the lee of the summit, watching the mujahideen striding past and calling us to follow, we basked in the thought that we had conquered the fourth and reputedly most difficult pass of all. Then, rather as if he were opening another bottle of champagne to celebrate some particularly splendid victory, Charles produced yet another large bar of mint cake, the last. Restored and almost drunk with joy, we set off downwards. It was a long, long, exhausting scramble.

At the bottom we stopped for tea beside a stream and reached our night-stop, the village of Gamma, at 4.45, fourteen hours after starting. The houses here presented a curious sight, their flat roofs surmounted by sugarloaf-shaped mounds of winter fodder. They looked snug and solid, ready for winter. The village mosque was not very big and by the time we, our equipment and a dozen or more mujahideen had moved in, space was very cramped. Charles was feeling unwell so he went to bed while the rest of us made for the tea-house a hundred yards away. There, after the usual Afghan delay, we treated ourselves to the luxury of milk tea and a very good hard, local cheese, rather like a French Tomme de Savoie.

It was so good that we ordered a second round, careless of the expense. I suppose the whole meal cost about £2 or £3 for six. It was only a flea-ridden wooden hovel with a dirty carpet on the floor, but it seemed splendidly cosy and comfortable. The milk tea and grilled cheese – rather like a raclette, which we ate with a pinch of salt and a piece of bread – were more satisfying than the most expensive meal I have ever eaten. We took some cheese back for Charles, who luckily was feeling better. By this time, 8.30, I could hardly keep my eyes open and I crawled into my sleeping bag with that sense of utter satisfaction that only physical exhaustion seems to bring.

16

Next day was 13 October and, although not a Friday, it did indeed turn out to be a day of ill omen. After an hour or so we came to a fork in the trail. Ahead of us, perched on the side of a steep hill, was the village of Papruk; to the left, the path dropped to the river and continued on the far side. Rahman and Nur made for the river, despite shouts from Stéphane that we needed provisions from the village. Two locals confirmed that the way to Papruk was straight ahead, but Rahman, in a thoroughly recalcitrant mood, ignored Stéphane's appeals and drove the horses across the river. Tom now entered the fray, shouting at the top of his powerful voice, 'Rahman, come back, you bloody fool.'

'Easy, Tom,' I pleaded, 'for God's sake.'

We were all furious at Rahman's bloody-mindedness, but could not risk being separated from the rest of the horses. After some difficulty crossing the river, we caught up with him a few hundred yards further on.

The argument blazed up again, Tom and Rahman snapping at one another like dogs spoiling for a fight. Eventually it came to a head. Rahman, his eyes bursting out of his head and shouting incomprehensibly in Farsi, picked up a large stone and made a rush at Tom. I threw myself forward and wrestled desperately with him. Although much shorter than me, Rahman was very strong and it was all I could do to hold him. Behind me, Tom was turning the air blue with military language and threats of what he would do to Rahman if he ever got hold of him. With Nigel struggling to restrain Tom and me fighting to pinion Rahman's arms, the battle swayed backwards and forwards for several minutes, until I managed to force Rahman to drop the stone. Panting, we finally separated the contestants and resumed our march. Rahman was still simmering like a kettle that may boil over at any time, and strode on ahead, leaving us to find the way as best we could.

We had only gone a few hundred yards when we came on him, deep in conversation with a local. This in itself was strange as until now Rahman had avoided contact with the Nuristanis, believing that they were all thieves and cut-throats. I could not make out whether Rahman knew this man, but they were clearly in league. Ostentatiously swinging a heavy stick, the man approached us and announced to Stéphane that we would have to pay a tax of five thousand Afghanis (£50) per horse to cross Nuristan. Otherwise, he said menacingly, he would put us in jail. It was clearly a put-up job but he looked a nasty piece of work and it was hard to know how far he was prepared to go. Stéphane squatted down beside the two of them and tried to argue reasonably.

'Go away,' said the Nuristani. 'You are an infidel. You stink.' This was the first time I had heard this insult used face to face. Stéphane was angry but managed to hold his ground without losing his temper and eventually the man got bored with the charade and we were able to go on. Nur looked highly embarrassed and was clearly torn between his sense of responsibility for us and loyalty to Rahman, a co-religionist.

We completed the rest of the day's journey in a state of uneasy truce, reaching the bottom of the valley and, to our surprise, the first road we had seen since leaving the Panjsher. This led to the village of Pul-i-Rostan (Bridge of Rostan) distinguished by the beauty of its mosque: one side stood open to the river and was adorned with beautifully carved wooden pillars. Prayers were in progress by lantern light and we had to wait outside in the darkness until they had finished. Eventually they brought us dinner from a nearby house, cheese and oil, chicken and rice and tea.

In the morning I woke to find someone kicking my foot. It was the mullah come to say prayers at five. He was obviously angry at finding our infidel legs in the way and we had to move, so as not to offend the faithful. However, my irritation at this intolerant behaviour evaporated when a hearty breakfast of eggs and milk tea arrived. While the horses were being saddled up I saw some boys playing a kind of golf, with sticks and a ball of twine.

'Might I try?'

They willingly handed me club and ball and I gave it a clout. To my chagrin one small boy consistently hit it cleaner and further than I did. But who would have thought to find the game of golf – or was it hockey – being played outside a mosque in the wilds of Nuristan?

Leaving the young golfers behind we rode up the valley coming, in an hour and a half, to a village called Nikmuk (pronounced Nick Muck) and describing itself as the administrative capital of Nuristan. To prove it, the little square in front of the most official-looking building was defended by two or three ancient machine guns (they looked like Maxim guns from the 1880s) and a group of elders carrying *jezails* (long-barrelled rifles) approached to meet us. They turned out to be friendly and invited us to tea. We had no real choice but to accept, although we were impatient to get on and we regretted our decision when the tea had still not arrived after half an hour. We did, however, decline an invitation to stay for lunch and very reluctantly the good citizens of Nikmuk let us continue to the next village, Barg-e-Makal.

The houses in these villages were the most elaborate we had seen, the woodwork of the eaves and doorways being beautifully carved in geometric patterns. It was a delightful afternoon ride, much of the way on the flat alongside the river. We had dismounted in one meadow for a rest when Stéphane rode up to say that there had been an accident with the camera and that Tom and Rahman were half a mile behind. Charles and I immediately set off on foot and found Tom by the side of the path, trying to dry out the camera with his handkerchief.

'What happened?' we shouted.

'The horse went in the river to have a drink and when Rahman tried to drive it out, it went in deeper and nearly drowned. The camera was under water for two or three minutes. Got completely soaked.'

'Is it ruined?' I asked.

'I don't know. I'll dry it out and have a proper look tonight.'

Rahman, curiously, seemed to have forgotten his violent quarrel and was eager to help. After ten minutes we loaded the damp camera back on the horse, which until now had seemed the surest-footed and most reliable beast of all, and rode on, reaching the village of Avzai as it was getting dark. Frustratingly, we seemed to be making slower and slower progress.

The owner of the Avzai *koffi* came bustling down the steps of his ramshackle wooden house like a Dickensian inn-keeper, full of oily welcomes. The room above looked exceptionally dirty, even by Afghan standards, but at least it had two chairs and a table on which Tom now spread out the complicated electronic innards of the camera to dry. We had finished filming, so it did not really matter whether the camera worked or not, but what did worry me deeply was whether the tapes, in which was invested our entire documentary effort, were surviving the terrific pounding of the journey.

Next morning as we saddled up, another group of mujahideen *en route* to Chitral appeared and breakfasted in the field beside us. It was another sunny morning and as we rode on up the valley the yellows of the walnuts, mulberries and willows vied with one another for sheer brilliance. In the miniature fields, the harvest was still being gathered in, and lines of tiny wheatsheaves were neatly laid out to dry.

We reached Peshawarak, the last big village in Nuristan, at lunchtime and once again, although we were keen to press on, Rahman and Nur elected to stop. Rahman argued that here we could find food for the horses and ourselves, and by making an early start, we could scale the last pass in one day. I knew this meant another of his famous mystery marches in the dark, but once again felt that, since we certainly could not cope with the horses on our own, we must humour his whims.

Peshawarak (not to be confused with Peshawar in Pakistan) was another attractive village, with a finely carved mosque and some handsome house fronts. We were installed in a small room belonging to the tea-house, with a single window looking on to the village square. As we sat on the floor with our backs to the wall, waiting for our lunch, the room went dark. I looked round and found two or three locals leaning on the window sill staring at us with silent concentration.

'Go away,' Nigel shouted as if shooing a hen. Reluctantly, they removed themselves, but a few minutes later they were back again. Afghan inquisitiveness is incorrigible.

In the afternoon we watched the locals playing *buzkashi*, the national game, in which two teams of mounted men fight for possession of the 'ball', a headless calf. To score a goal the calf has to be dropped in a small circle. In Peshawarak this was just under the grandstand – the top of someone's house. The game started with both teams racing at full gallop the length of a big meadow and back. They then milled about below us, struggling for possession of the calf, until finally one rider managed to wrench it away from the others and drop it in the circle to score. I could see that not only do the players have to be exceptional horsemen, but they also need to have amazingly strong arms. Afterwards we watched the top scorer's horse – the size of a polo pony – being elaborately rugged up under the admiring gaze of the villagers. This was only a local game: the real thing, as played in the north and Kabul, must be as exciting as a cavalry charge.

We rose early and left at three. As I had anticipated, we blundered about in the dark, twice losing the path, before coming to the bottom of the pass. By six, however, we were well on our way and at eight we came to a sheep shelter and decided to boil our kettle for tea. We had bought some hard cheese in Peshawarak and that, with fresh melted butter and bread, made a very passable breakfast. Rahman was up to his old tricks, sitting off to one side in a huff and refusing to eat. When we asked why, Stéphane translated.

'He says you have not washed your hands before eating and that therefore the food is unclean.' To show solidarity, Nur joined him in his hunger strike. I thought it was pure hypocrisy; I was pretty sure they had not washed their hands either.

So there we were, facing the final pass, our spirits correspondingly high, despite the continuing row with Rahman. We set off at about eight and climbed steadily, the path zigzagging up a shoulder, bare except for an occasional wind-bent, dwarf cedar. We reached the final steep ascent to the summit unexpectedly quickly. I stopped for a rest, panting. Stéphane, Tom and Nigel were near the ridge, easily distinguishable from the fifty or sixty mujahideen who were walking with us. A grinning group passed me and waved at me to come on. Charles was about twenty yards ahead and I forced myself into motion again, not wanting the gap to become any greater. As I neared the top, another group of mujahideen sprinted past me and, laughing, a boy of about twenty turned and held out his hand.

'Here,' he said, 'let me give you a hand.' (At least, I guessed, that is what his Farsi meant.)

'It's all right,' I panted. 'I'm fine.' But he insisted, grabbing me firmly by the wrist and towing me up the last twenty yards to the top, where the others were waiting.

'We've done it,' Charles cried. 'The last pass.' Unfortunately we had eaten all the Kendal Mint Cake so our celebration had to be purely spiritual. I stood on the ridge, fifteen thousand feet up, and gazed at the mountains of Pakistan in front of us. Turning for a last look at Afghanistan I saw a solid phalanx of snow-capped peaks; the great massif of the Hindu Kush rose ridge after ridge to the far horizon.

We set off downwards with a glowing sense of achievement, which not even a sharp snowstorm, driving bleakly into our backs, could altogether dampen.

There had been much discussion as to how we should best cross the border to avoid any trouble with the Pakistani police. At first it was thought that we should go over at night, when they would all be asleep. But when it became clear that we would be travelling with a big party of mujahideen, who would give us a kind of protective colouring, a daylight crossing seemed less complicated.

A few hundred yards before the border village, one of the mujahideen stopped me and, standing on a rock beside the path, wound several yards of smelly turban round my head in an effort to disguise my Britishness. It was to no avail. When we reached a bit of stony path, near the farm which was decreed to be the border, we were immediately intercepted. A tall Pakistani policeman stood in the middle of the crowd of Afghan mujahideen, peering about as if he were searching for something.

'Inglistan,' I heard him say, his eyes darting about. Then he looked straight at me and, unimpressed by my turban, cried: 'Inglis, Inglis.' Tom, Nigel and Charles were similarly spotted, the policeman becoming more and more excited. Only Stéphane escaped detection. He now said that Rahman, whether out of panic, stupidity or malice, had certainly not helped our cause by volunteering to the policeman that he was escorting a party of four Britons and one Frenchman. 'Bloody Rahman,' we swore. But it was too late now.

We were handed over to a falsetto-voiced man who led us down the valley on what turned out to be an interminable last hike. We reached Garm Chisma, all bustle beside its grey-green river, at five, fourteen hours after leaving Peshawarak. Hundreds of pack horses and mujahideen milled about, jamming the single street. At Jamiat headquarters, a rambling tea-house, fellow Panjsheri drivers greeted Rahman and Nur, throwing their arms round them and hugging and kissing them. Crates of AK47 rifles wrapped in greaseproof paper (I guessed from China or Egypt), lay half open in the courtyard. A constant stream of mujahideen, mainly from Badakhshan, pushed their way in and out.

Falsetto-voice disappeared and another furtive-looking policeman took his place. He tried to give Tom a chunk of hashish which Tom politely declined, thinking it might be a plant. On reflection, it was probably just Pakistani *politesse*.

Were we under arrest or not? It was hard to make out. The local Jamiat men tried to reassure us that as soon as we got to Chitral everything would be settled in a trice. But when we arrived there the following day, in the unaccustomed luxury of a jeep, this proved to be wishful thinking. We were taken first to police headquarters – another relic of the Raj – and then to the office of the Resident Magistrate, who turned out to be a smart alec with, he said, a place waiting for him at the London School of Economics. He was anxious for us to sign an affidavit saying that we had crossed the Pakistani border clandestinely – a suggestion which Nigel and I rejected vociferously. We finally settled for a more anodyne phrase and returned to the office of the Police Superintendant, who told us we would fly to Peshawar the following day – the ticket cost £6 – taking a policeman with us as escort: we would, of course, have to pay our escort's fare.

We reassured ourselves that once we reached Peshawar we would have no more trouble, and repaired to the 'best' hotel in town, the Trichmir View, so named because it had a spectacular view of the snow-capped mountain range of that name. I imagined that in British days it had been a delightful colonial-style hostelry, with no doubt a motherly if autocratic *memsahib* in charge. Now, alas, it was about the dirtiest and most ramshackle hotel I have ever been in, and apart from ourselves was empty. The manager was an Afghan, with an unshaven chin and a greasy look. My room, when I was shown to it, had no bathroom. I protested to the manager, who told me airily that I could use the shower at the end of the corridor. It was in the same room as the lavatory and when I turned it on, it showered the whole room, including the lavatory seat, with cold water.

I felt this was a disappointing return to civilization, but consoled myself with the thought that tomorrow we would be in the great city of Peshawar. Dean's Hotel now assumed the sort of aura that normally one associates with the Ritz in Paris, the Plaza in New York or the Carlton in Cannes.

It was a superb flight, and we all sat on the edge of our seats like schoolboys, watching the mountains unfold below us, laughing at the thought that we did not have to climb another single pass. The rather serious young policeman, very neat in his blue uniform, sat behind us impassively. We had told him that we intended to go straight to Dean's to unload all our luggage before going to police headquarters, and he politely agreed.

As soon as we reached Dean's, I telephoned the British Embassy in Islamabad and asked for my friend, Peter.

'Peter,' I said, 'we're back. All in one piece.'

'Thank God,' he said, 'We were getting a bit worried about you. That's very good news. Did you manage to make your film?'

I told him that we had had some pretty terrible problems, but that we had managed in the end.

I added, 'One thing. We seem to be technically under arrest – in fact we're on our way to the police station now and wondered if you could pass the word . . . '.

'Yes,' he responded, picking it up at once, 'we'll get on to the Foreign Ministry at once.'

'It might be worth a call to President Zia's office,' I suggested.

'Unfortunately,' Peter interrupted, 'he's in China. But don't worry, we'll do the necessary at this end.'

The first police station sent us to a second police station, CID headquarters, where the Deputy Commissioner himself took over.

'Where have you come from?'

'Chitral,'

'But before that, you were in Afghanistan?'

'Yes.'

'In Kabul?'

'No, no, we were in the Panjsher Valley, with the mujahideen . . . .'.

'Pan . . . What is the name of that valley?'

It went on like this for at least an hour. Tea was brought, and then more questions. The Commissioner looked in and had a rapid and unintelligible conversation in Urdu.

Finally, the Deputy Commissioner, an agreeable, polite man with, I discovered, a passion for cricket, asked, 'May I have your passports, please?' We handed them over.

'You are staying at Dean's?'

'Yes.'

'We'll take you back there.' He fixed me with his eye. 'Can you come here tomorrow at ten?'

'Yes, I suppose so. You understand we are very anxious to get home. . . '.

He raised a soothing hand. 'Of course, Mr Gall, I quite understand. Just a few more formalities and we will wish you God speed.'

When we were back at the hotel, Charles said, 'I've got another passport.'

We looked at him with amazement. 'How come?'

'Oh, one I had for the Middle East, I think it was. . . '.

'Come on,' I said, the idea already full-blown, 'let's find out the time of the next flight to London.'

It turned out there was a flight that night, but from Karachi, and the plane from Pershawar to Karachi left in an hour. Charles packed in ten minutes and we spurred on the old taxi driver from the hotel to drive at top speed.

We arrived with barely half an hour to spare to find an enormous crowd blocking the entrance to the airport.

'What the hell's this?' Charles cried in despair.

'The haj,' the old taxi driver croaked. 'All the pilgrims coming back from Mecca.'

We fought our way in, Charles clutching the kitbag full of tapes while I lugged his suitcase. I had reasoned that it was just possible that the Pakistani police might confiscate our tapes in order to see what we had been filming. If that did happen, it was equally possible that we would never see them again. And even if we did get them back, I was afraid they might damage them. We were already concerned that we had a fault called 'drop-out' on some of them. So it was wise to take no chances. But now, another hold-up occurred. The customs man insisted on inspecting Charles's suitcase. As the minutes ticked away, he rummaged deeper and deeper, pulling out shirts, socks, underwear. . . .

Furious but helpless, Charles hopped from foot to foot, fuming, while I wondered what would happen if the customs man wanted to see inside the kitbag. For some inexplicable reason – possibly because it was hand baggage – he did *not* want to see the kitbag and with only minutes to spare, Charles ran up the steps to Departures, turned and waved, and was gone. I returned to Dean's to have my long-anticipated and much-desired hot shower, the first for nearly three months. I could hardly believe that the simple act of standing in a bath with hot water pouring over my body while I soaped myself with a thoroughness, which I hoped would drive out even the hardiest of Afghan lice, could give me such immediate and complete pleasure. Before dinner, Nigel, acting as treasurer, splurged £25 on a bottle of local Murree Whisky, a passable imitation of the real thing, which we drank in the cheerless atmosphere of the Permit Room – the only place in Pakistan where intoxicating liquors may be consumed. Our long-planned celebration dinner of tomato soup and chicken tikka tasted as ambrosial as imagination had promised, but maybe the Murree Whisky had something to do with the euphoria of our first night back in civilization.

The Deputy Commissioner never knew that Charles – and the tapes – had gone, although the conversation took a tricky turn the following day at headquarters.

Just as I was wondering what was coming next, the Deputy Commissioner leaned forward.

'Did you see the match last night?'

'The what. . . ?' I stammered.

'The cricket. The Test. Last night on television?' (Pakistan were playing the West Indies.)

'Oh, no,' I said. 'Was it good?'

'First-class,' he beamed. 'Absolutely first-class.'

I knew then that we would be all right.

AFTERWORD

When I got back to England, I weighed eleven stone, a stone and a half lighter than when I had set out three months earlier. I looked and felt emaciated. The documentary *Afghanistan: Behind Russian Lines* was edited and on the air in five weeks, which was extremely fast work. It went out at 9.00 p.m. on 23 November 1982 on ITV and, thanks to an enormous amount of pre-publicity, had a very big audience for a documentary – 7·6 million viewers, exactly the same as the BBC's Nine o'clock News that night. *Behind Russian Lines* was widely acclaimed, but I was more impressed by the scores of letters that I received from ordinary people saying how moved they had been by the programme and enquiring how they could help: many asked where they could send money. I replied to all of them, suggesting that they could send money or other gifts to the Afghanistan Support Committee in the Charing Cross Road.

I also received a very special letter from our old friend, Mohammad Es haq, in Peshawar:

Dear Sandy Gall!
    I'm happy to wrote you. I was eager to know what you have done. When I heard you lost your camera I was sad, but when saw your film I said it worth taking such a risk.

Dear Sir,
    From material gain point of view definitely you lost a lot, but you contributed a great deal to a noble cause which was about to be forgotten. I saw the film and showed it to others. Everybody liked It. It is a real achievement for your. Your film like a stone dropped in pool of water creat waves which will neve vanish and continue to stimulate peace loving

peoples' feelings all over the world for a long time. Now we consider you and your crew as our sincere friends and of depressed people of Afghanistan and your name and your face with bautiful white hear will be remembered long in the future.

You are a wose man and you know our problems and situation, so there will remain no room for our excuse if anything unfavorable has been committed from our side.

Your Mohammad Es haq   27-12-82

About the time that Es haq was writing to me, the Russians launched their third offensive of 1982 against the Panjsher, accompanied by intensive bombing. But for some reason that was not immediately clear, they withdrew after a brief and apparently unsuccessful stay. Then a strange thing happened. Reports started filtering out of a ceasefire in the Panjsher, coupled with suggestions that Masud had done a deal with the regime in Kabul. The most extreme version, which appeared in some newspapers, was that Masud had opted out of the guerrilla war altogether. I could hardly believe that, since it would be totally out of character for him and completely at variance with everything we had seen of the mujahideen themselves in the Panjsher.

I imagined that if there had been a deal of some sort, Masud had entered into it for tactical reasons: that his plan was, as the French would say, '*reculer pour mieux sauter*'. Now, seven months later, every sign points to this being the correct interpretation. He has put to good use the breathing space that the truce allowed him, settling old scores in the neighbouring valley of Andarab to the north, where a strong Hisbe faction was preventing supplies of food getting to the hungry population of the Panjsher. One night, I am told, Masud went over the high pass into Andarab (he would have gone by the same route as we had taken to Parende, on our way to meet the dashing Gulai Dar), surrounded the offending village and disarmed its menfolk at dawn; an impressive operation that left him master of this fertile and strategic valley.

I do not know when he will eventually move over to the attack again, hitting the Russians in their bases, as he predicted to us so vividly, sitting cross-legged in the corner of a crowded room one night in the Panjsher. But he is, by all accounts, as full of fight as ever and as determined to drive the Russians out of his country.

Will the West help Masud and the Afghans in their struggle for independence? Will it help them *enough* to resist the Russian juggernaut? That is really the question to which we, as democrats, should be addressing ourselves. I believe it should. Self-interest alone should be enough to make us see that. If the Russians become more and more painfully bogged down in Afghanistan, as seems likely, they will be less likely to launch into fresh adventures in other parts of the world. But there is the moral argument as well. Should not we in the West, who have the good fortune to belong to the Free World, support other peoples who are fighting for their freedom? Especially when they are fighting the most ruthless imperialist power in the world today, the Soviet Union. And if anyone doubts that, let him go and spend a month in the Panjsher, or Herat, or Kandahar and watch the Russian bombs falling on the villages of Afghanistan.

And should not the Western media start reporting the war in Afghanistan on a proper, full-time basis? Not just now and again when some freelance manages to get some shaky footage of a mujahideen attack. Should not the war correspondents be there, as they were in Vietnam and the Lebanon? I think the editors who make these decisions should wake up and do something about it. No man is an island, as we all know. The death of an Afghan child in some remote mountain valley diminishes us all. The destruction of an Afghan village by Soviet bombers should anger us all.

Guernica shook the world and moved Picasso to a masterpiece. Who is going to make the world weep for the Panjsher villages of Rokha and Bazarak, Astana and Jangalak, Omarz and Shawa? Who will weep for Tambonnah and Tunkhu and Abdullah Kheil? Nobody, if no one reports the terrible things that are happening on the other side of the mountains.

Byron gave his life on the battlefield of Missolonghi in the cause of Greek independence. Perhaps there are no more Byrons about today, so let the last word lie with an Afghan poet, Hanzala of Badghis who lived in the ninth century.

> *If leadership rests inside the lion's jaw,*
> *So be it. Go, snatch it from his jaws.*
> *Your lot shall be greatness, prestige, honour and glory.*
> *If all fails, face death like a man.*

Penshurst, May 1983